To my grandfather Robert Townsend

For building the past

CONTENTS

Illustrations vii

Preface.. ix

Introduction.. xii

Chapter One: Private Albert A. Windsor 1

Chapter Two: Corporal John F. Austin 5

Chapter Three: Private Abel B. Kenyon 41

Chapter Four: Corporal Charles P. Nye 45

Chapter Five: Sergeant Charles F. Colvin 59

Chapter Six: Private William H. Jordan.......................67

Chapter Seven: Private William O. Harrington 71

Chapter Eight: Roster of Company K 133

Bibliographical Notes 153

About the author 155

ILLUSTRATIONS

State of Rhode Island in 1862 xxi

Captain George N. Durfee 12

Corporal Charles P. Nye 47

Benjamin W. Pendleton 51

Sergeant Charles F. Colvin 61

Colonel Zenas R. Bliss 68

Harrington Farm...113

PREFACE

On September 6, 1862 the Seventh Rhode Island Volunteers was mustered into the service of the United States for three years. The Seventh was incorporated into the Army of the Potomac and joined the First Brigade, Second Division, Ninth Corps. They would fight with this unit from the horrors of Fredericksburg to the garrison of Fort Hell before Petersburg. Along the way, the regiment fought engagements in Mississippi and Kentucky and would return to Virginia in 1864. Here the Seventh Rhode Island Volunteers would face constant danger from Spotsylvania, to the North Anna, Mechanicsville, Cold Harbor, Petersburg, and Poplar Spring Church.

This study was first begun when in 2001. Tramping through the woods of western Rhode Island, I was drawn to the hundreds of small, historic cemeteries that dotted the landscape. Abandoned to progress, the small marble and granite monuments stand in silent testimony to those who went before. On the stones of many Civil War veterans are inscribed the unit they served with. Many of the headstones I located were carved, "Co. K, 7th RI Vols." Further research indicated that this company had been recruited in the area I now traversed. As I began the research for my book, *The Seventh Rhode Island Infantry in the Civil War*, the men from Company K again appeared. This time not as statuary in the woods, but through their words, written on long ago faded pieces of paper. I discovered six sets of letters, nearly all of them interconnected. I knew that I had an interesting story to follow. That tale is one of many chronicled in my regimental history; the effect of the Civil War on Rhode Island through the study of one regiment. This book follows that band of Rhode Islanders as they recorded the war as seen through their own eyes.

The Seventh Rhode Island was composed of ten companies, which were recruited from throughout Rhode

Island. One of these was Company K. These men were typical Rhode Islanders, working the hardscrabble farms and textile mills of their native state. Company K was recruited in large part from the western Rhode Island towns of Coventry, Scituate, and Foster. In addition, ten men were drafted from Company A; men from south-western Rhode Island to bring the company up to its required strength. These men were typical of the soldiers that joined the Seventh. Most were in their twenties and some were married.

The company was the basic building block of the infantry regiment in the Civil War. At full strength it mustered 100 officers and men; a regiment with full ranks was 1,000 strong. By 1863 most companies mustered only thirty men. Companies were usually recruited in the same community. These soldiers fought together, side by side in two ranks. Men who had known each other all of their lives in small country villages, and had never gone to Providence, now found themselves facing death together on the battlefields of the south. The bonds that were in place before the war, remained in place during it. Instead of breaking and running to the rear, these men stayed and helped each other carry through the death struggle. Those bonds of community never disappeared, except by death, which was a frequent and common occurrence. While the soldiers gave much attention to their comrades, there remained those at home. These letters were sent to alleviate tension and to let "the folks" know that all was well, in addition to passing along the news from the front. When the carnage was over, the volunteer soldiers simply returned to their farms and shops and continued on with life, as they remembered those who paid the ultimate sacrifice.

When Company K left Providence on that September day in 1862 its ranks were nearly one hundred strong. When they were mustered out on June 9, 1865 the casualties suffered by this one company were appalling. Ten fell in battle, seventeen perished from illness, while medical discharge and resignation took another twenty. Twenty-two were wounded in action. In addition, seven more were transferred to the Veterans Reserve Corps; only three soldiers deserted. In total one hundred and ten officers and men served in Company K. The company suffered a sixty-nine percent casualty rate, while a quarter of the men died in two years and nine months of service. The Seventh Rhode Island Volunteers would lose 227 men in their service. The losses in Company K would be felt severely in the close knit hamlets with names such as Hopkins Hollow, Moosup Valley, and Rockville.

Prior to the Civil War, Rhode Island was experiencing a revolution in education. A basic schooling was compulsory, and both boys and girls took the opportunities to learn. The men of Company K have left behind a rich legacy through their letters. Found in collections throughout Rhode Island, they tell the story of this infantry company in the Civil War. Through their preservation over the generations the men of Company K continue to speak. Their letters tell the story of the Rhode Island soldier during the most critical moment in the history of the United States. From the faded words come rich descriptions of many aspects of service in the Federal Army, coupled with moments of sheer terror experienced during battle.

This work is the result of many contributions from the people of Rhode Island. Without them this work would have never been possible, for in the one hundred and forty three years since the Civil War ended, they have carefully cared for the written words of the veterans of Company K. First and foremost are the many groups and individuals who graciously allowed their material to be transcribed and presented in this volume. These include the Rhode Island Historical Society, Pawtuxet Valley Historical Society, Foster Preservation Society, North Scituate Public Library, Kris VanDenBossche, Loren Andrews, and the Matthews family. In addition, the following individuals have all contributed to this project in many different ways: Craig Anthony, Mike Lannigan, Shirley Arnold, Mark Eddleston, Joyce Knight Townsend, Dr. J. Stanley Lemons, and Katie McDonald.

    These letters have been transcribed exactly from the originals. No spelling or punctuation marks have been added. When the soldier misspelled the word beyond modern comprehension, the intended word has been added in parenthesis. Many times in their letters the soldiers would speak about their comrades. In this manner, this editor has freely used William P. Hopkins, *The Seventh Rhode Island Volunteers in the Civil War: 1862-1865* to provide background information on the soldier, in addition to the campaign the Seventh Rhode Island was engaged upon when the letter was written. This also includes information pertaining to the men mentioned in the particular letter. This writer has included photographs taken from Hopkins' book to illustrate the men in Company K. These letters provide the reader with an insight into one company of infantry in the Civil War.

                                                Robert Grandchamp
                                                Warwick, Rhode Island
                                                September 17, 2007

INTRODUCTION

On May 22, 1862 Governor William Sprague issued General Orders Twenty-Two for the raising of the Seventh Rhode Island Volunteers. This regiment was to be the last three year infantry regiment to be raised in Rhode Island. Camp Bliss was erected in southern Providence and was to be the destination for the recruits for the regiment. Hundreds of men came to Camp Bliss in the summer of 1862. Some were Mexican War veterans, or had seen service in the United States Army and other volunteer regiments. Some were politicians and gentlemen from the hierarchy of the state. The majority were fifteen to thirty year old farmers and mill workers from southern and western Rhode Island whom enlisted in the regiment under the call of President Abraham Lincoln for 300,000 men to defend the Union following a series of humiliating defeats in Virginia. The largest push for recruits came in August, with some towns offering incentives as high as four hundred dollars for men to enlist; though the large bounties encouraged many to come forward, the main ideal calling men to fight was patriotism. There was a large threat that the United States would be destroyed forever. Many of the officers attained their positions through political influence or past experience in the service; fewer than half had seen any service. In two months one thousand young Rhode Islanders had gathered at Camp Bliss. To command them, Governor Sprague selected Zenas Randall Bliss of Johnston. Bliss was a graduate of West Point and had attained the rank of captain in the Eighth United States Infantry. In the years ahead he would transform these men from Rhode Island from untrained volunteers into a combat regiment on par with the United States Regulars.

    The Seventh Rhode Island was mustered into the service of the United States to serve for three years on September 6, 1862. They also drew Enfield rifle-muskets. In addition the Seventh was clothed in the full uniform of the United States Army; a feature of the coats being a very high collar. On September 10, the regiment left Rhode Island and proceeded to Camp Casey outside of Washington D.C. Here they remained for several weeks before joining the First Brigade, Second Division, Ninth Corps on October 6, camped outside Sharpsburg, Maryland following the victory at Antietam a month earlier. The Seventh remained encamped at Pleasant Valley, Maryland for three weeks, perfecting its drill, while losing several members of the regiment to disease and the elements.

In late October the Army of the Potomac again embarked upon another campaign to capture Richmond. In early November, Ninth Corps commander, Major General Ambrose Burnside assumed command of the Army of the Potomac. On November 15, the Seventh fought its first engagement, holding a key bridge against Confederate cavalry. Later that month they arrived at Fredericksburg, Virginia. The city lay in the path to attack Richmond. Burnside waited for over two weeks for pontoons to allow his army to cross. The result would be the near destruction of the Seventh Rhode Island.

The Army of the Potomac had to attack across a wide open plain to reach a Confederate division entrenched behind a sunken road. In addition, Marye's Height contained twenty-four pieces of artillery. The Seventh Rhode Island went in at 12:20 on the afternoon of December 13, 1862. Almost immediately, Rhode Islanders were being killed and maimed. Lieutenant Colonel Welcome B. Sayles was hit in the chest by a shell, sprinkling pieces of his body all over members of the Seventh. After halting in the middle of the field to fire their Enfields, the Seventh surged forward in an attempt to flank the wall; they were repulsed by "a perfect volcanoe of flame." They stopped fifty yards from the sunken road. The Seventh's flag became the farthest advanced banner in the Ninth Corps. After remaining on the field for seven hours, the Seventh was relieved and returned to Fredericksburg. Five hundred and seventy officers and men went into the fight, two hundred and twenty became casualties; including forty-four dead. As the regiment assembled after its charge, Colonel Bliss said to his battered regiment Rhode Islanders: "You have covered yourself with mud and glory." Bliss would be nominated for promotion to brigadier general and receive the Medal of Honor for his actions. Many of his enlisted men would receive promotions for their actions on the field.

Following the Battle of Fredericksburg, the Seventh Rhode Island returned to its winter camp across the Rappahannock River near Falmouth, Virginia. Here many of the men would experience the hardships that their ancestors experienced at Valley Forge some eighty-five years earlier. Food and money was scarce, while typhoid, dysentery, and pneumonia reduced the regiment even further. Even in the worst of weather, one company of the regiment was constantly on picket duty along the river. A respite came in mid-February when the Ninth Corps was transferred to Suffolk, Virginia. From here they were again transferred to Lexington, Kentucky when Burnside was given command of the Army of the Ohio.

In June of 1863 the Seventh left Cairo, Illinois as reinforcements for Ulysses S. Grant's army as they besieged Vicksburg, Mississippi. They spent two weeks entrenching around Vicksburg before being sent to Jackson, in order to prevent Confederates from reinforcing the Vicksburg garrison. Here they defeated the Rebels at the Battle of Jackson. Though the Mississippi Campaign only lasted two months, forty-five Rhode Islanders lost their lives. In August they were recalled to Kentucky. The Seventh entered Mississippi with slightly over three hundred men; over half would be infected by disease. Yazoo Fever, dysentery, and typhoid reduced the regiment to mere company strength.

They spent a miserably cold and wet winter as the provost guard in Lexington, Kentucky, where they protected the loyal citizens against John Hunt Morgan's Confederate guerillas. Furthermore they completed a fifty mile march in the dead of winter to guard a remote outpost along the Cumberland River. Following this, the regiment was again summoned to Virginia in April of 1864 as reinforcements to the Army of the Potomac. At this time only two hundred and fifty men were on duty.

The Seventh returned to Virginia and crossed the Rapidan on the road to Richmond. They were held in reserve at the Battle of the Wilderness on May 5-7. Yet were heavily engaged from May 12-18 at Spotsylvania Court House, all the while fighting in a driving rain. On the eighteenth the regiment found itself cut off and surrounded; a desperate bayonet charge was ordered. It failed and shattered the confidence the men had in their new commander. From this day on the Seventh was engaged in combat continuously. They fought at the North Anna River on May 25. On the third of June, the Seventh charged the Confederate line near Bethesda Church; one third of the regiment went down. In mid June they arrived at Petersburg, Virginia with only one hundred and twenty-five men. As they were constantly under fire, nearly one Rhode Islander was hit each day. On June 20, 1864 Company H mustered one man present for duty; only two commissioned officers were left and eighty men remained. With such a reduced number men, the Seventh Rhode Island was pulled off the line and acted as engineers for the Second Division, Ninth Corps. Colonel Bliss was thrown from his horse at Spotsylvania, so Percy Daniels, who had bungled the bayonet charge at Spotsylvania, was commissioned as lieutenant colonel.

On July 30, at the Battle of the Crater, the Seventh supported the main attack, providing covering fire as the Ninth Corps withdrew from the failed mission. They remained in the entrenchments throughout August and

September. On September 30, 1864 the Battle of Poplar Spring Church was fought. Here the Seventh again showed its mettle by stopping the stampede of the Federal army as the Confederates bore down upon it. In November they were consolidated with the Fourth Rhode Island Volunteers. In addition, men returned to the front and some recruits arrived from Rhode Island.

    In November, the regiment moved to Fort Sedgwick, also known as Fort Hell as it was the closest fort at Petersburg near the Confederate line. The men lived underground in shelters known as "bombproofs" to escape the murderous fire outside. The Seventh remained here until April 2, 1865 when they were amongst the first to storm into Petersburg. The resulting campaign ended with the pursuit of Lee to Appomattox Court House. The original regiment was mustered out of the service on June 9, 1864, while the recruits were mustered out on July 13, 1865. 1,145 men served in the Seventh Rhode Island, 227 died.

    On March 13, 1865 General Ulysses S. Grant formally gave his permission for the Seventh Rhode Island to paint the following engagements upon their colors where they had fought and died: Fredericksburg, Vicksburg, Jackson, Spotsylvania, North Anna, Cold Harbor, Petersburg, Weldon Railroad, Poplar Spring Church, and Hatcher's Run. When the Seventh Rhode Island assembled for the last time on June 21, 1865, Colonel Daniels addressed his men one last time. He said, "Abraham Lincoln never called truer men to defend our flag then those who have fought under the colors of the Seventh Rhode Island Volunteers."

September. On September 30, 1864 the Battle of Poplar Spring Church was fought. Here the Seventh again showed its mettle by stopping the stampede of the Federal army as the Confederates bore down upon it. In November they were consolidated with the Fourth Rhode Island Volunteers. In addition, men returned to the front and some recruits arrived from Rhode Island.

    In November, the regiment moved to Fort Sedgwick, also known as Fort Hell as it was the closest fort at Petersburg near the Confederate line. The men lived underground in shelters known as "bombproofs" to escape the murderous fire outside. The Seventh remained here until April 2, 1865 when they were amongst the first to storm into Petersburg. The resulting campaign ended with the pursuit of Lee to Appomattox Court House. The original regiment was mustered out of the service on June 9, 1864, while the recruits were mustered out on July 13, 1865. 1,145 men served in the Seventh Rhode Island, 227 died.

    On March 13, 1865 General Ulysses S. Grant formally gave his permission for the Seventh Rhode Island Volunteers to paint the following engagements upon their colors where they had fought and died: Fredericksburg, Vicksburg, Jackson, Spotsylvania, North Anna, Cold Harbor, Petersburg, Weldon Railroad, Poplar Spring Church, and Hatcher's Run. When the Seventh Rhode Island assembled for the last time on June 21, 1865, Colonel Daniels addressed his men one last time. He said, "Abraham Lincoln never called truer men to defend our flag then those who have fought under the colors of the Seventh Rhode Island Volunteers."

"It was a sad time any way we can fix it such a time I never want to see again but verry likely we shall see more fighting if we do I hope the Lord will be with us and carry us safe through & be permitted to return home once more and see you all again."

–Private Abel B. Kenyon
December 26, 1862

RHODE ISLAND TOWNSHIPS - 1862

CHAPTER ONE

Private Albert A. Windsor

Albert A. Windsor was an eighteen year old farmer from Foster, Rhode Island who enrolled in Company K on August 16, 1862, and was mustered in on September 6. Albert's letter was written as the Seventh was just settling into the Army of the Potomac at Pleasant Valley, Maryland. He seems, to have enjoyed the life of a soldier, declaring it "tip top." This letter was addressed to his sister Mary who also resided on the family farm, located near the Danielson Pike.

Pleasant Valley
Saturaday Oct 18th 62

Dear Sister
      I thought I would pen you too let you know that we are here alive and well tough and strong we are in the same place as we were when I wrote last monday I suppose you have got that letter by this time we have not got any mail since last tuesday night there was none for me then they say they are a comeing to night and I am looking for our next mail we are under Burnsid now I se him yesterday he had on an old black hat and an blouse and the same old Horse he had in the mexican war he looks as bad as a privat you would not know him from a private if it was not for his

Shoulder straps[1] and Hardly then does not go out in fine clothes Enos[2] is a standing guard to day I expect to stand to morow we are under marching orders so we are likely to move any time I am fleshy and well now, I have been down to do my washing to day I guess you would laugh to see me a scrubbing but I got my shirt quite white I have nothing to do to day they don't drill saturdays they let us do our washing and clean up every saturday I have not heard from Searls + Adin[3] for some time they are at Frederic yet the rest of the Foster boys are all well that come from around there I was over to the 4th R. Island + the 11th Ct the other day and I see George Douglass he was well and I see Aseal and Shade Simmons and Bill moary[4] they are well they have been in several fights tell Olney and Jeremiah that Ozial is well and sends his love to you and to Jeremiah he said he was a going to write you a letter afore long and to Jeremiah to I will tell you what I had for my supper last night rice and molases coffee and hard bread for breakfast I had som more rice and coffee and fried bacon which was tip top I have not got louses yet but I expect them every day there is plenty of men encamped around here we heard guns the other day in the vicinity of charlestown there was one man killed and 2 wounded so they say some times the war looks so it will close soon then it will look more gloomy we had quite a rain Thursday night it wet through our tents at first but soon lightened and stopped wetting though we took it very lively

---

[1] Many soldiers would describe Major General Ambrose Burnside in this way.
[2] Enos Farrow of Foster died in Washington on December 3, 1862 of typhoid.
[3] Searles B. Young of Foster was wounded at Fredericksburg and discharged the following February. Adoniram Hopkins of Foster was discharged for disability in March of 1863. Both men were left at Frederick, Maryland suffering from typhoid fever.
[4] These regiments were encamped near the Seventh. These men are not identified.

we laid down and covered up and we to singing happy as a clam I am In a tent not with tom, Henry S. and Ashel+ Jim Bunn and a fellow named Thurston[5] I think I shall go into a tent with Enos and George Sim mmons+ Shippee[6]

    look on the other sheet

This is the second part as there is olney three in there and they want me to move in with them I though at first I should finis on one sheet but kept a thinking and a writing I have just got my dinner down I had bacon and hard bread and beans but the beans I don't eat I suppose we would get tired of hard bread but I suppose it goes better than you would suppose when they are good sometimes we get mouldy ones than they go back to the quarter master very quick and we get good ones for them if there is any in store John Austin is not very well I don't know what the matter with him the weather is quite mild now it is warm days and cool nights now there has been no frost yet out here houses are rather scarece they are mostly old Fashion I should like to be at home to se the folks once more we have 60 rounds of cartridges 40 in our cartridge box and 20 in our Haversack I want you to write all thing that would suit me about the affairs around their while I am writing they tell about that battle that I heard the guns of the north lost only 1 man killed the south lost between three hundred and 4 killed and about the same taken prisoners I hope that it is true I don't think of much more now to write I am a going to place this letter in the mail but I don't know when it will go so you can direct

---

[5] Henry S. Cole of Foster was killed at Fredericksburg. Asel Hopkins of Foster died of disease in Tennessee on April 11, 1864. James A. Bunn of Glocester survived the war. Caleb Thurston of Richmond was discharged on February 29, 1864.

[6] George Simmons of Foster was killed on May 12, 1864 at Spotsylvania. Horace J. Shippee of Foster was mustered out on June 9, 1865.

the letters the same as before so if we should move from here they will follow us I shall write if we move as soon as I can I want you to write soon I have got paper enough but no postage stamps now I will close yours & A.A. Windsor

Private Albert A. Windsor was killed December 13, 1862 at the Battle of Fredericksburg

CHAPTER TWO

Corporal John F. Austin

Corporal John F. Austin was twenty-one years old and a carder at the Ashland Manufacturing Company when he enlisted in Company K on August 8, 1862. Austin lived in the village of Ashland, located in western Scituate. He resided with his wife, Emily, brother in law Pardon Bennett and Emily's mother. Austin joined Company K, with several other men from Ashland. His letters convey a husband away from his wife for the first time, learning to do many skills, while missing her immensely.

Letter I. *Following his enlistment on August 8, Austin went to Camp Bliss, located in Cranston, Rhode Island. Here with his fellow Scituate soldiers he learned the basic maneuvers of Casey's Tactics. Though he only left Scituate, some ten days earlier he already missed his family.*

Camp Bliss Aug the 23 1862

Dear wife
               I now take my pen in hand to let you know how we are getting along I am well at present and hope that these few lines will find you the same I like camp life first rate we have plenty to at and to drink you aught to have been heare yeasterday to see the man waking up and down before the tents with a barrel over his head and another was riding on a rail half a day we expect to bee examened to day they wer here to pay us but we were not payed yet but i think we

will.[7] know to day who is going to washington tell your mother i should like to see her and all the boys give my love to all the folks and tell then that i should like to see them all i canot write any more at present so good bye write son and often

>from your husband
>John F. Austin
>Direct your letters to
>Camp Bliss Co K
>7th Regt R.I.V

Letter II. *Upon arrival at Camp Bliss, the recruits were given a medical examination by Albert Cummings. Corporal Austin was described as standing five feet four and one half inches tall, and had blue eyes, brown hair, and a light complexion.*

Camp Bliss Aug 25th

Dear wife since i sent the letter this morning i have been trained and passed the doctor here and so i am contented now and i think you had better come down next monday and get some money i can write any more as i have to send this by Mrs. Horas Patterson

>From you husband
>John F. Austin

Letter III. *The Seventh Rhode Island left Camp Bliss on the afternoon of September 10 and proceeded on a multi-train and boat journey to Washington. The Seventh settled into Camp Casey, near Alexandria and began to learn the drill that would transform them from volunteers into soldiers.*

---

[7] The men were examined by Albert Cummings, a doctor from Providence. As he had enlisted from Scituate, Austin received a bounty of four hundred dollars.

Washington DC Sept 12th 1862

Dear
   Wife I now take my pen in hand to let you know how i am getting along i am well at present and hope that you are the same we have got in camp at last and it seems rather more like home we are campt at the capitol hill in sight of the capitol of Washington City the capitol is one of the handsomes buildings that i have ever saw and i wish that you were heare to see it the boys are all in good health and spirits and like verey wee we had a good time coming out hear the boys say that they would like to go back to philadelphia and see some of these girls there as they are all black out heare but some of them are pretty good looking girls tharre is in sight of us campt on every hill and every piece of level ground in sight and almost every train of cars that comes in brings a new regiment of soldiers thare camps on every side of us tell the boys that i should like to see them all but i do not want to come back to Ashland till we git old Jeff Davis tell Albert and Williams Rhodes[8] that i am going to write to them in a few days as it took us till late last night to get our camp up but never mind we shall be all right. In a few days tell Mother and alvira that i should like to see them this morning and i think i shall come over this evening and see them Emily i am looking at you as you read this letter and can see you as you run over the lines but i never wish to fare any letters than since i left home and i want you to give yourself no worriness about me on account i am sitting on my napsack with my paper and my pen wrighting to you the one i love the best of all on earth and i hope that in a few month to return to my home and see those i lov there wright to Mother and let her know how i am gettin along i am going

---

[8] Albert and William Rhodes lived in Ashland and worked at the Ashland Manufacturing Company.

to wright to them in a few days and so i mus bid you good bye dear Emily so heare I one kiss for you i want you to write as soon as you get this as i do not no how long we shall stay here

>Direct your letters to
>Washington DC
>7th REG RIV

Letter IV.

Washington DC Sep the 16 Saturaday

Dear
Wife i now take my pen in hand to let you know how I am getting along i am well at present and hope that these few lines will find injoying good health we arived in Washington Friday night about 10 clock all safe we had a good time coming out heare after we left the boat we went on the cars to groton then we took the boat to new york from new york to philadelphia and we took supper thiere and staid their about two hours and we had a good time for there are lots of handsom girls their to recive the soliers and you must not be pelious if i tell you that we shook hands with all the girls in the place and kiss them besides i am writing to you sitting on my knapsack not far from the capitol we had to camp out doors last night and i slept as sound as tho i had ben at home and i never fared better in my life than when i was coming out here give my love to them

not write till we get settled down

so good by John F Austin

Letter V.

Arlington Hights Virgina

Sept the 18th 1862

Dear wife I now take my pen in hand to let you know how i am getting along i am well and as hearty as can be and i hope these lines will find you the same since i wrote to you we had orders to march from capitol hill and we were ready to go any where so we straped on our napsacks and struck our tents about 3 oclock and started for where we did not know but we marched 6 miels and crosed long bridge the bridge was 1 mild long and are now camped in virgina and since we went in to camp 7 or 8 regiments come on camp on the same ground the 6 Battry[9] is in camp close to us i have been up there and see Lester Hill[10] he is well and tuff as ever most of the boys are well but some of them got tired marching up to Arlington Hights but i stood it first rate and i like this country first rate one of the boy tool a rebel close by here and feched him into camp the other day and he was a shabby looking fellow he was out as a spy there is new regiment coming in here every day and in every directin is an incampment so we have plenty of company and are not lonesome at toll we are in general Pauls brigade and in Caseys division[11] there is four regiments of us together all encamped on the same ground we heard that they got the news in rhodes Island that the 7th regiment was all cut to pieces but we are all together yeat and in good spirits and ready to meet the eneny if they come where we be for we have got plenty of forts to help us where we be now and 2 Battrys now an plenty of troops coming in every day give my

---

[9] Battery E, First Rhode Island Light Artillery. Also called the Sixth Battery. Many Scituate men served in this battery.
[10] Lester Hill was a resident of Foster and a corporal in Battery E, First Rhode Island Light Artillery. He later became a lieutenant in the 14th Rhode Island Heavy Artillery.
[11] Brigadier General Gabriel Paul commanded the brigade, while fellow Rhode Islander Major General Silas Casey commanded the division.

love to them all and tell them i should like to see them i have not wrote to any of the wrest of the folks yet as i have not had time mooving aroud as i have been i want you to write to the folks in foster to William or Mother and tell her son has not forgotten her yet and that he will writ as soon as he gits time and git settled down in a place to stay any time tell William Rhods that he aught to be out here for we have some bang up times out heare and tell Albert the same and that i wish he was out heare with me it will pay a fellow if he lives to get home if he did not fare so well as he did at home but we have fared so well so fare seeing how much we have moved Emily i know not hardly what to you but time passes swiftly out heare and i hope still that i may live to see your face again and to imprint on your face again another kiss so I must bid you good by for this time Emily from you love John F Austin
Direct your letter to Arlington Hights VA
7 REG. RIV in care of Cap Durffey[12]

Letter VI.

Arlington Hights Sep the 19th 1862

Dear

Wife i now take my pen in hand to let you know how i am getting along i am well at present and hope that these few lines will find you injoying the same health i have been out this forenoon looking around I have a better chance then when i was down at Camp Bliss the Corprels have to go off with the men after some water so I got some sweet potatoes and boiled them for my dinner I have charge of 16 men and they are all good fellows and we buy things to

---

[12] Captain George N. Durfee of Little Compton was the first commander of Company K. He was only eighteen when he became captain. Durfee resigned his commission March 20, 1863.

geather out heare the news are quiet good about this time out heare to day the news came into camp that Mac Cland[13] had given the rebels 4 hours to surrender but they say that they will not so they will have to fight it out Emily i have writen 3 or 4 letters and have not recievd any yet i want to heare from you to send me some 3 cts postage stamps as i cannot git them out here as i write these lines i am still thinking of the Emily but i am would not have you think that i am homesick at tall for i live as well as i wish to out heare but some of them think that if they do not git every thing that they have at hope that they fare hard but i do not find any fault yet and am not agoing to till they hang me i like it first rate the weather is warm out heare days and cool nights Emily i have to look at your face every day and i can see how you look as you are going around Ashland tell your mother that i send my love to her and all the rest of the folks around there Emily I must give you another look so good bye for the present do not forget the stamps

Be sure to Direct your letters
to Washington DC 7th REG
of RIV. Co K
You can send me a box now if you wish to now i should like to have you send me a box of cigars from the store
   from your affectionate husband John F. Austin

Letter VII. *On September 17, 1862 the bloodiest day of the Civil War was fought at Antietam, Maryland. The Union Army declared it a victory.*

Arlington Hights Sept 21th 1862

---

[13] Major General George B. McClellan, the commander of the Army of the Potomac.

Dear wife i now take my pen in hand to let you know how i am gitting along i am well at present and hope that these few lines will you and the rest of the folks I recived

Captain George N. Durfee

your letter and was glad enough to heare that you were all well it see like words that you were speaking to me at home everything goes on well heare now and i thing that they are diggig wells and gitting lumber for a barn i think that we shall stay heare all winter but we cannot say tell it will be some things go along in the army if we keep on gaining victorys i think we shall be kept heare as a reserve for the City of Washigton there is about two hundred thousand troops about Washington and 40 to 50 thousand camped in sight of us the news are very good now out heare it is not of much use for me to rite any peticuulars as you git the news almost as quick as we do out heare Emily i want you to write to me as once a week and i will try to answer them for to heare from them that we so dearly love gives in new life and energy and i still hope and trust that the days will soon come that we shall see one another and talk face to face once more but if i never see you again theare hope that i shall meet you again in a better and Happier land wheare theire will be no more wars and no more fighting Emily I mus bid you good bye this time as i was on guard last night and am rather sleepy i want you to not be troubled about my not have enough to eat for we have all the salt horse that we want and good white bread and soop and i like it first rate so hear good luck to you Emily from your husband John F Austin

Still i think of thee Emily Although i am far from thee

Letter VIII.
Arlington Hights Sept 27th 1862

Dear
Wife i now take my pen in hand to let you know how i am getting along i am well at present and hope that these few lines will find you the same i recived your letter of the 23 and was glad to heare from you and others that you was all well Emily I should like to see all once more and i think that the time is not far distant when peace will once more reign over this land and we shall return to our homes to injoy the company of those that we love but i may be mistaken but i think that by spring we shall return to our homes the rebels talk of sending comishioners to Washington to settle peace by that will not come of they want a separation of the states i have not much to write as i have written almost every day we are all well and injoying good health i should like to see you all you rite that you see in the paper that we have not moved from Arlington Hights and i think that we shall stay heare all winter you must send

me something for i should like to see smething that comes from home you nead not be afraid to send a box any time to me for I shall git it if you direct it to me the same as you direct my letters if we should move at all come to me if you direct my letters if we should move it will come to me if you direct it to the 7 REG RIV Washington Dc i cannot write much more to night i have just recived your letter and am answering it to night this ink is some that we make to day so we thought that we have made to day so we thought we would try it so i must bid you a good night Emily so heare is another kiss for you but do not like the way of kissing by letter i had rather have your own face i think it would be better

From your affectionate husband
John F Austin

Although i am far away my thoughts are still of thee Emily

Letter IX.

Arlington Hights Sept the 29

Dear

Wife i now take my pen in had to let you know how i am at present and hope that these few lines will find you the same we are orded to march but we do not no wheare they say we are going to Fredrick city so i thought i would rite you a few lines and let you know that we wer going away Emily so not be scared at this for as quick as i get where we are going i will write you another so Emily i must bid you good bye as it is about time for us to march and i cannot tell what well our next stopping place Emily tell them that i give my love to them all write the same as ever to the 7th REG RIV and i shall get your lettrs so Emily good bye

From your husband
John F Austin

Letter X. *On October 3, 1862 the Seventh Rhode Island received orders to leave Camp Casey and march to Pleasant Valley in Maryland. It was here that the Army of the Potomac was encamped following the hard fought victory at Antietam. The Seventh would also confront its first battle with disease.*

Fredrick City
Oct the 2 1862

Dear
Wife I now take my pen in hand to let you know how i am at present and hope that these few lines will find you the same since i wrote last time i have taken a quit a ride we left Arlington Hights Monday in the afternoon and went to Washington and staid all night and sleep out doored on the ground and i had a good sleep but for the feathers lays rather hard the next morning we took the cars for Fredricks City we were on the cars all day and night and since we have got heare the regiments have been coming in every train of cars i heard that the 11 RI REG had arrived in Washington and that they were coming out[14] but i do not no certain i do not think that we will stay heare long but i do not know how it will be i like first rate out here better then i did at Arlington Hights this morning i went into a mans potatoe field and got some potatoes and fried them with some poark and we had a good breakfast we expect to move again from heare right off i heard that we weres going with Burnside and

---

[14] The 11th Rhode Island remained in the Defenses of Washington throughout the winter of 1862. In the spring they were transferred to the Peninsula of Virginia. They only fought in one small skirmish and were mustered out in June of 1863.

i hope at is so for he is a good man the city where we are now is a handsome city i have been all over it i went up their after i got heare and to a private house and got some hot coffey and pies and hot biscuit and butter and some peach preserves and all we had to pay was 25 cts and that is the cheapest meal that i have bought since i left Rhodes Island you ought to see the rebel prisoners heare in the city there is a lot of them that were wounded in the battell a few days ago some of Jacksons army passed through the city but were soon put to flight by our men there is a great many seems to be seem in a soldiers life i cannot tell them all now but if ever i get home i shall have enough to tell you all there are things that are to good to write now Emily i should like to see you and all the folks around Ashland but i do not care to come fore anything else but to see those that i love sometimes my thoughts run back to the home that i love so well and thoes that are deare to me there but if i never see that home again i hope that i shall live so that i shall meet you all in a better land than this but i would not have you think i am atall down cast i am sorry that i ever done i had rather be in the army today than to be doing nothing around home i have seene a great deale since i have been out heare Emily i cannot write any more i want you to rite me every day if you can for it gives me so much pleasure to heare from home so heare is a good kiss for you my wide from your husband J F Austin

Letter XI.

Harpers Frey Oct 8th 1862

Dear
Wife i now take my pen in hand to let you know how i am at present and hope that these few lines will find you the same since i wrote you to you before we have marched from Fredrick City to Harpers Ferry we have

camped up in the mountains 3 nights wheare it was as steep as the roof of a house we sleep up about two hundred feet high in the mountains above us is another peak of the mountain as high as the other and i have been up on the top of it and looked over on the other sid and see the army on the other side we are camped on the ground where the rebels camped a few weeks ago and we are with burnsid now and hope soon to give the rebels what they do not gut every day our folks are giveng them good work and i hope that it will continue so our troops keep coming in almost every day Old Lincoln was bye heare the other day and he says that he will have us home in 6 months but i think that we will git home so soon as that we have not got our letters since we left Fredrick city but i have got all the rest that you rote to me and i think that we shall git them as we have got in camp again Emily i should like to see you gan and the rest of the folks but i like heare the first rate Burnside howle army have just marched in heare and we have got order to march again but i do not know wheare we are agoing and it does not make much differance if we can only meet thee fir one more for i think that we will give them fits this time Emily i had a letter from Pardon but i have not had time to answer it yet but will try when to answer it as soon as i can we are all marching so much that i can hadly git time to write to you the one that i feel most bound to write to you it is that i love thee best of all Friday has just come to my tent and wants to give his love to Clarke Allen if he is at home and the rest of the folks around these and he says that he should like to have holt of Sam Allen that he would give him a good shaking give my love to the boys and tell them to bee good boys and take good care of there mother and control themselves at home for there is many hardships to be endured in the army marching about from place to place but when we are in camp we have a good time tell mother that i send my love to her and that i should like to see heare i send my love to you all

Emily and must bid you good bye for this time so heare is the kiss for you this time i wish that you would send me a box but do not know but you have but i have not recived any yet so good bye JFA.

Letter XII. *The Seventh remained at their camp near Sharpsburg throughout October of 1862.*

Camp near Sharpsburg Oct the 13 1862

Dear

Wife i now take my pen in hand let you know how i am gitting along i am well at present and hope that these lines will find you injoying the same blessings it had been some time since i had heard from home and i began to think that i should not git any more letters but last night was Sunday night and the mall bag came with a full load and i got your letters one was the 29 the other the 7 and you aught to see the boys there neer was a more pleased lot of boys i think in my life every one was glad to heare from there friends that are fare away i never thought that i should injoy myself so well in reding letters but when one has been so long from those dear frinds that he so much loves at home a sad fealing comes over them of they do not heare often from them as i write to you i often think how you will like to heare from me and i can imagine how you look at home as you gather at the fireside at home to read the letters i write to you i can see you around the old kitchen fire at the table i can see you Emily as you are going to and from the mill i know that you miss me from the family circle but not more than i miss the fond inderments of hime an the society of those frinds around home but i hope that the time is soon roling on when we all shall see each other and shake the fredly hand togeather again the troops keep coming in all the time and i that if we could all engage the Rebels once more that we could about forc the thing to a close but i dont now how it will be it is all gods work yesterday we heard the firring of canon all day they were fighting somewheare about 20 miles from heare but i have not yet heard what place it was i could not help smiling when i opened that long letter of yours dear Emily to see how much pains you took to write me such a long letter but as i read over the lines i could not but help weeping for my thoughts strayed back to the dear one that pened those lines to me and thought of how i should like to see you all tell the boys to take good care of the things and be good to the mother that is left to us at home tell her that i have not yet forgoten her and that i should like to be there and take dinner with her and i hope and i think that i shall come back to see you all buy life is not a shure thing as we all know but let us hope for the best but if i never meat the family circle at home may i meat you all in a better land but i must now change the subject of this letter you wanted to send me a box Emily i have looked for one many a day but we are apt to get disapointed some times and i should like to have you send me one as quick as you get this letter i should like to have some good cackes and pies they will not be long coming out heare as many have had them sent and you need not fear any trouble about it coming through i had a letter from William O Sweet and one from William Rhosed so i had a good lot of letters to read i was glad to heare that you were lonsome is not any doubt but i want you to go home as often as you can and cheer up miss Matheson and all but i want you to keep the most yourself Emily from John F. Austin

Letter XIII.

Plesant Valley Camp near Sharpsburg Oct the 13 186

    Dear

Brother i now take my pen in hand to let you know how i am getting along out heare i am well at present and hope that these few lines will find you the sam i recived your letters and was glad to hear from you and that you had got a chance to go to work i have recived all the letters from home now an i was glad to hear that they was all well there Pardon i like very well out heare i have enough to eat when we are in camp but when we are on a march we hav nothing but hard bread and meat that goes first rate when a fellow gits hungry we have fresh meat soop and sometimes we fryed Pardon you should have seen us when we wer up in the mountains about 200 feet high we sleept up there 8 nights and abov that it was about as again and i went up there and looked over on the other side and see the army on the other side and it was a grand sight the 7th regiment is in Burnsides division and camp near Sharpsburg Maryaland the news are good out heare now we are in good health and spirits and ready for action Pardon i think that you have got to carrying the girls around constrable and i expect to see you keeping house where i com home so i can come and see you and your and you little wife around there gitting me a good dinner but you must be good to mother and help her all you can till i get home again if i ever do but i canot tell how that will be but we must hope for the best and trust in the futur Pardon you would like to see me writing to you on my napsack to night i often think of you and the home that i love so well but i enjoy myself out heare as well as i can and that time hass swiftly away out heare and think that by spring the war will be nearly at an end and we shall all return home that live to see more to night so i must bud you good bye in the present from your brother

John F Austin

Letter XIV.

John F. Austin

Oct the 15 1862 Camp near Sharpsburg

Dear
Wife i know seat myself to pen you a few lines i am well at present and hope that these few lines will find you and the rest of the family well it is with pleasure that i seat myself this morning to write to you we do not have much to do now so I cannot think of much to write to you at present but we injoy ourselves as well as we can but it is of the that i am thinking of now at home and the loved ones that i have left there but i do not regret that i have come out heare to help to relive this our beloved land from the hands of thoes that are trying to destroy it and i think that before the spring time dear Emily comes again that this war will be brought nearly to a close and that thoes that live till that time will return to there homes to once more injoy the comforts of the loved ones at home Emily my heart often yearns towards home and i think of you talking there but i had rather you would not work in the mill but you can act at your own pleasure about it i want you to not deprive yourselve of the pleasure of goin around I want you to go and come just the same as if i were there go up and see mother as often as you can and tell her that i still think of her daly as i go about my duties as a solder ther is not many that can more appreciate the joys and comforts of home than those that are deprieved of the privlage things are very high held in Maryaland you can not bye much of anything at all cheese is 25 cts a pound molasses is $100 a gallon and every thing in propotion but we are git along very well we have fresh meat two or three times a week we have some good bread and some of it has been maid so that we have two stones to break it up but we have had enaugh to eat you write to me to write to you about

how George Hopkins[15] lost his money i do not know how he lost it i am shure but he felt very bad about it and i was sorry when he lost it Emily you must keep up good courage for i think that it will not be many months before we shall be at home tell Albert and alvisa that i send my love to them and that i should like to see them and tell mother Bennett not to take to much snuff till i come back to see her tell her that i should like to sit down to her table with them all once mor and eat a good dinner tell the boys that i should like to see them all tell Edwin not to git marrid till i get home for i want to go to the weding and Nathan the same Emily there is not much more room on this sheet of paper so I shall have to draw this letter to a close so heare is a good kiss for you Emily good bye from your husband John F Austin

Letter XV.

> Pleasant Valley M D
> Oct the 19 1862

Dear

Wife i now take my pen in hand to let you know how i am gitting along i am well at present and hope that these few lines will find you and the rest of the folks well i recived your letter of the 13th and was glad to heare that you was well i recived one also from Pardon dated Oct the 12th i wrote an ansar to the one that he wrote before and directed it to Crompton[16] for i thought that he was agoing there to work to day is the Sabbath and i am seated again trying loved ones at home to write to the i think as i am seated this morning hear in a distant land of the many pleasant sabboth mornings that we have spent togeather at

---

[15] George Hopkins resided in the village of Clayville. His son Darius was in Company K; Darius died of disease at Camp Denison, Ohio on September 29, 1863.

[16] A mill village in Warwick, Rhode Island.

home and how we have injoyed ourselves walking over the fields and i wonder to myself sometimes if i shall ever injoy those privagles again and i cannot help thinking but what i shall return again to the loved ones at home and again enjoy their comforts and happiness once more but i will leave that to another being who is mightier then me Emily i can but help thinking of you this morning how i should like to be there with you all but neverless some it cannot be we must make the best of it and when i do return if ever i do i hope there will be nothing more to separate us till death shall come but i will turn to other things the boys are all well and send their love to you George Hawkins[17] is a cooking for our boys now and they all like him first rate John Studley[18] is tuff as can be and is full of fun as ever you wanted to know why there wives not gut more letter i guess george does not write so often as i do but John writes letters somewhere every few days Friday[19] is in the tent with me now and he is as noisey as ever and just as tuff you keep writing about sending me a box there has been some sent and we have to send an order to Washington to git them i want you to send one and see of you can git it there is a man gone after what has been sent but he has not got back yet i guess we can git them well enough Emily i can not think of much more to write at present but i want you to be a good girl till i come home tell mother Bennet how i should like to be there and plague her a little while to day but i will be there sometime and make it all up so here is a kis for you from your husband John F. Austin.

---

[17] George W. Hawkins of Scituate enlisted August 14, 1862 and was mustered out on June 9, 1865.
[18] John N. Studley resided in Ashland and was a friend of John F. Austin. He was wounded at Fredericksburg and was discharged on April 3, 1863 at Providence.
[19] "Friday" is clearly a member of Company K, but his identity is unknown.

Letter XVI. *As Austin remained in the army, he learned many skills that he would not have known if he remained in Ashland. Without their wives present, the men were required to learn such vital skills as cooking and repairing their clothing. Austin and the men continued in a variety of fatigue duties and prepared themselves for the coming cold.*

Oct the 25 1862 Maraland
Camp near Pleasant Valley

Dear

Wife i now take my pen in hand to let you now how i am gitting along i am well at present and hope that these few lines will find you and the rest of the folks the same george Hawkins says he wrote to Nathan that i was sick i was troubled with the disantary for a few days but i have gott well again[20] and am hearty and i feal better then before i recived all your letters now today Henry Searls[21] had a letter and he said that you wer finding a box for me i shall look for it now Emily i should like to see you once more and all the rest of the folks at home but i dont know when that will be i hope in the spring we are going to march tomorow to harpers ferry acrost into Virginia the longer i stay away the less i think of it but from my thoughts they mane is never absent and thy love is ever hovering around me you aught to have seen me cooking griddles cakes out in the woods without any thing but salt and flour and a little Coald watter to make them up[22] with Emily when i get home you will have nothing to do as i can cook and wash now for i have been out today

---

[20] As the Seventh remained at Pleasant Valley, many of the men began to contract diseases such as typhoid and dysentery.

[21] Henry E. Searle was a resident of Scituate. In 1865 he was transferred to the Veterans Reserve Corps. After the war he became a Baptist minister in Foster.

[22] Also known as "Johnny Cakes," a dish well liked by Rhode Island soldiers.

washing my close for it is Saturday and we having nothing else to do Emily i should like to have those blue pants and shirt and cap that i left at home boxed up and sent to me if it does not cost you to much to send them and a pair of mittens or a good pair of gloves would be better for me on account of handling my gun send the can that i got up to Richmond if you send any you can sent them to me i will save my drawing any for sometime and then i shall have a good amont due me ahead Emily i send my love to you tell mother that i am coming home to see her in the spring if i live till that time i am in such a hurry to day as we have so much to do to get ready to move you must excuse the writing of this time and as soon as i got moved again i will rite to you Emily hear is another kiss for you i do not like them but i like the old way that we use to kis from your husband

John F. Austin

Letter XVII. *On October 27, McClellan finally put the Army of the Potomac on another campaign to take Richmond. This was the first march that the Seventh Rhode Island engaged upon and many of the men found it a hard campaign. However it would be nothing compared to the campaigns in the years ahead.*

Camp near Lovetsvill VA
Nov the 1 1862

Dear
    Wife i now take my pen in hand to let you now how i am gitting along i am well at present and hope that these few lines will find you and the rest of the folks at home the same i have just recived another letter from you and was glad to hare that you are all well at home we have been marching on with Virginia we have crosed the Potomac and advanced about 17 miles into Virginia we had a pretty hard march I

can tell you as we now have out tents to carry on our backs now but i stood it like a brick and i am tuff as can be i can eat freed bacon wheare it runs a lone but we do not have such meat as that that all the time we have good fresh beef 3 times a weak and we can fry it or make it up to a soap and it goes first rate i can eat a good lot of it any how we are camped in a good place now it is as pleasant as spring and the trees have not yet lost thear leaves and everything is as lovely as can be i like to wander through the groves heare and sometimes wish that you were by my side to wander along with me it the most splendid place that i ever saw there is some of the handsomes farms that ever i saw almost think i should like to live heare my self one day to day is Saturday and i have been to the river to wash up and i see 4 rebels spys that our men were hanin in they looked rather motly as they were riding by they take them almost every day now heare you said thatyou want me to answer pardons letters i have answerd 2 that i have recived and tat is all that i have recived from him tell him not to be offended if he does not git them very often as we have much to see to now i can hardly git time to rite to you every day almost we have to git ready to march and sometimes we go and sometimes we have to unpack again but we are advancing on toward the rebel lines and the hole army of the potomac is pushing on we have somewhere about 10 thousand with our division and as many more ahead of us and still they keep coming all the time such sights as pases heare every day one would tink that we could not help whipping them this time i have not yet got the box but i think that i shall get it very soon as they have gone after them Emily i think i make it suffer i canot write any more at present so heare is a kiss from the pen of your husband JFA

Letter XVII

Nov the 7 1862
On the march to Richmond
Dear
    Wife i now take my pen in hand to let you now how i am gitting along i am well at present and hope that these few lines will find you the same since I last wrote to you we have been marching every day we have had long and hard marches some days we have marched form 15 to 20 miles and carried our knapsacks and i began to think milirary is rather hard work but i have stood it just first rate so far and i hope that i shall be well and stand it through our company has been out on picket duty and we fared first rate we killed 1 hog and 3 ducks and some chickens and 1 turkey and we had plenty of fresh meet to eat that night and since we have been marching we have had plenty of fresh meat to eat so we have not fared so very bad yet when we were on picket the major[23] came around and told us that the rebels wer 2 miles off and that we must keep a good lookout for them so we had our guns all loaded redy for them but they did not attack us we have drove them back all the time and they go so fast that we can not keep up with them so i do not no where we shall come up with them they do not like to stand before our army now they say that we have 800 thousand troops all moving now and i think that we shall see or heare of a hard battle now before long it is snowing to day as i sit wrighting and i am thinking of the loved ones at home and that i should like to see you all again but i shall have to stop riting at present Emily for we shall have to march again to day Emily heare is the same kiss for you so be a good girl till i come back again so good bye as i am in a hury to day from

                                                  your husband
                                                  John F. Austin

---

[23] Major Jacob Babbitt of Bristol was mortally wounded at Fredericksburg.

Letter IXX.

Sulpher Springs V A Nov the 13 1862

Dear
         Wife i now take my pen in hand to let you now how i am gitting along i am well at present and hope that these few lines will find you the same we have been marching now for 16 days and all we stop is over night in a place and to day while we are resting i will write you few lines but i shall have to write in a hurry s the guard is going out in a few minuts i have recieved 2 letters the other day and was glad to heare that you was well at home i write to you to send me some money but i have not got any yet i want you to send me some in a letter for when we are marching i should like to have it to bye things to carry with me as we have got out of hard bread now but we have meet enough to eat now you can send the mittens by mail the other day we were drawn up in line of battle and some of the boys were sick right off we were where we could see the cannons fire and heare the troops as they yeled and charged on the rebels but we drove them back with out any loss and nobody hurt Dear Emily you must ecuse me for not wrighting any more this time for we are in a hurry this time when i git stopped for a while i will rite you a long letter so the boys are all well but rather tired from there long marches but a few days rest will make them all right again Emily heare is my love for you and all the rest of the folks at home and a kiss for you so good by for this time

from your affectionate Husband
John F. Austin

Letter XX. *On the morning of November 15, Companies C, D, and I of the Seventh under the command of Captain George E. Church fought a small skirmish with JEB Stuart's*

Confederate cavalry near Warrenton, Virginia. The companies held a bridge against the cavalry and saved the Ninth Corps wagon train. Though he was not engaged, Austin's letter offers a vivid description of the skirmish.

Headquarters 7th Reg R.I. Vol., Col. Z.R. Bliss,
Company K

Camp near Warenton VA Nov 17 1862

Dear Wife i now take my pen in hand to let you now how i am gitting along i am well at present and hope that these few lines will find you the same and the rest of the folks at home enjoying the same blessing i recived your letter with the money in it yesterday and was glad to get it and to hear that you wer all well at home and you rite that you had all moved in to geather i hope that you will take comfort togeather now for i feal more contented to hear that you are all togeather for i think that you will not be so lonesome all togeather when we started from Sulpher Springs last Friday we had been out on picket and just as we got ready to start the rebels got two batteries on the hill abot where we wer garding a bridg and began to shell us but we got our batteries in place and we made them leave pretty quick i can tell you one of the companies that we left there was shelled and they left in all directions one man had his cap nocked off and another had his haversack off by a piece of shell but no one in the regiment was hurt i belive i understood that one of the batteries men was killed but i have not found out for certain but they fired away pretty smart for a while i can tell you i could hear the shells as they went whising over our head as the stood in the road a little ways off and they sounded pretty i can tell you and i thought that i did not care about there coming any nearer to me then they did but i expect that i shall soon heare them coming nearer but i hope not we are camp near the warington railroad now on a large plain there is 40 or 50 thousand men in this division and so i can see plenty of folks and we have plenty of company yesterday was the sabboth but it did not seem much like it as we had to march all day and we hardly know when Sunday comes at all as we have to march Sunday and all they say that Burnside is going to take his Christmas dinner in Richmond if his plans is not found out but i do not no how that will be but hope that it will be so send me some tobacco by mail as we can not git it out heare now send me half a pound at first and see if i get that for i would like to be there and end this war so we can come home in the spring i hope that he will be succesfull in his plane we recived a paper last night when we got into camp and the news seen very good and we were glad to hear the news boy holering once more i began to think that i had got home again Emily i should like to see you and all the folks at home once more and sit down at home and tell to you what i have seen and gone through with and i hope that the time will soon roll around when we shall meat to not be parting any more till death shall part us give my love to all the folks at home and tell the boys that i should like to see them all so heare is a kiss for you Emily John F. Austin

Letter XXI. *On November 25, the Army of the Potomac arrived at Fredericksburg, Virginia. At this time the city was held by only one small Confederate brigade. Instead of fording the river, Burnside waited while pontoons arrived from Washington. In the meantime, the Seventh encamped at the town of Falmouth, across the Rappahannock River.*

Fredericksburg Nov the 24 1862

Dear
   Wife i now take my pen in hand to let you now how i am gitting along i am well at present and hope that these few

lines will find you the same and the rest of the folks at home well we are camped before Fredericksburg yet and we are gitting rested now and i thought as i had not much to do i would sit down and rite you a letter for i dont no when i shall git another so good chance we have not taken the city yet we heare for some purpose but i cannot tell for what the troops keep coming in hear all the time yeasterday there was a large lot of cavalery passed heare and i guess that they are going to cross the rier heare pretty soon we have plenty of Artilery heare[24] and when we do begin to shell the city i think we shall give them good work but i think that they will leave the city before we have much fighting heare but I cannot tell much about it we throw a few shells once in a while at them but they do not seem to answer them yet but i expect that they are trying to get reinforcements but we have got a good force heare now and i think that we can stand them a pretty good pull anyhow i think that they will the 7 rhodes island boys on the other side of the river ready to recive them with a guranty of other troops ready to recive them and give them a warm welcome i think that before night we shall give them a try but i do not no for ceartain i have recived two letters now within a few days one with the money and the other with the dated the 17 i want you to write as often as you can if you do not recive many from me as we have to move so often that i think that i shall git uste to moving by the time that i git home for every day it is strike tents and git ready to move somewhere till within a few day we have got where we cannot git along so fast as there is some things in the way but we will clear the way pretty soon now in a few days you will heare of us marching along i hope Emily as i sit before my

---

[24] Fredericksburg would represent the greatest representation of Rhode Island soldiers in any battle of the Civil War. Under Burnside's command were the Second, Fourth, Seventh and Twelfth Rhode Island Volunteers and First Rhode Island Cavalry. In addition to Batteries A, B, C, D, E, and G of the First Rhode Island Light Artillery.

tent writing to you i think of you and the rest of the folks at home and of the many comforts that you are injoying i can see you as you are moving around home i can see you as plain as though i was there and sometimes i think that i should like to be there with you but not till i can come home for good and stay there and i think that this winter will settle it up i hope so anyhow give my love to your mother and tell her that i should like to sit down to her table once more give my love to the rest of the folks and tell that i am tuff yet so i must close my letter for this time so hear is a kiss for you John F. Austin

Letter XXII.

Fredericksburg Dec the 2 1862

Dear
      Wife i now seat myself to answer your two last letters which i recived with the gratest pleasure i am well at present and hope that this will find you injoying the same blessing there was a spell that you did not git your letters i think that they stoped them at Washington but now they seem to go as a regular as ever we git a mail every day or two and they come loaded with the things for us i got the last letter and the money looked old fashion as though they had just paid off there is not much news at present we lay hear a little way from the city and we are gitting pretty well rested again it seems old fashion to be heare in the camp again as we have to drill the same as when we were at Camp Bliss we are injoying ourselves first rate again the railroad runs but a little ways off from us and they bring in more food now than we had on them marches but what we are stoped heare so long for I cannot tell there is something going on somewhere but i dont no what the boys are all well that came from around there John Studley got his letters the same time that i did

mine and he got two dollars and so we are going off to have a spell you said that you are a going to send me some tobacco by mail and i am glad of that as it costs 2 dollars a pound out heare now there is only one or two sutlers and they ask what they are amid to for the things that they have but now the cars has got to runing things will be cheaper soon they ask 70 cents for a pound of cheese now and everything is high so that it will not take long to send a dollar but the most that i bye is meal for that goes the farthest of any thing that i can bye to make a journey cake and they good out heare meal is 5 cents a pint i am as hearty as a dog i can eat all the time i never was better in my life and i can only keep so i shall be all right but i can not think of much news to tell you at present i should like to have you send that blue shirt by mail and put in some envelops as i have got out and a few sheets of paper then tie up in as small a bundle as you can and not seall them up for they say that it does not cost as much where you tie them up with string Emily i am seated today out in the woods ritting to you by the side of an old stump choose that place for there i thought that i wold out of the noise of the camp and i could think of home and the loved one there and of the happy hours that we had spent togeather but still i drive those thoughts from my and think that the time will come that we shall injoy ourselves again more then ever we did before give my love to all from your affectionate husband yours forever

John F. Austin

Letter XXIII. *The pontoons arrived on the morning of December 11 and Burnside deployed his engineers to build several bridges across the river. The Seventh crossed and spent December 12 in a tobacco barn on Caroline Street. At 12:20 the Seventh was given the order to attack Marye's Heights. They had to cross an open plain to reach the hill. At the base of the hill was a sunken road with several brigades* of southern infantry; while on the hill were twenty-four pieces of artillery. The Seventh almost reached their objective, stopping fifty yards from the sunken road. The Seventh suffered two hundred and twenty casualties in less then seven hours of combat. Amongst the wounded was Corporal John F. Austin. Company K lost four killed and nine wounded. Austin was removed to a hospital in Washington D.C.

Washington Dec 17th 1862

Dear
      Wife i now take my pen in hand to let you know how i am getting along i am as well as culd be except be after being wounded my head is not very bad as the ball did not go very deep we had a hard fight of it i can tell you i did not see many of the boys as i was wounded when we first went on the field John Studley was wounded through the knee and i left him at the hospital on the old camp ground near where we fought he said that he was a gitting along very well i expect that you have ben anxious to hear from me but i could not get a chance to write to you before i have been sent to washinton and am in the hospital i have a good warm place to sleep clost to the fire and am quit comfortable now and i think we have a good man to take care of us i do not want you to worrey about me now for i am gitting along first rate and had rather be heare than to be in the battlels i want you to content yourself as we as well as you can for i am well as to my bodily health and i want you to send me some money and a box now that i am heare for i can gitt it now that i am heare send it right of as quicks as you git this letter Emily do not be frighten becaus your man has got a little scrath i think that he will come out all right in the end and word to my mother and tell her that i want a pice of cheese and i want

you to put in a piece anyhow and be shure to send it as quick as you can Emily i should like to see you and all the folks at home and i think i shall before a great while longer tell the boys that the rebels did not git me this time if they do not next i have got the ball that hit me in the head and i am going to keep it to remeber them by Emily it looks like home heare to see things that we can eat but we had a hard to git heare as we were about 3 days without anythings to eat but as soon as we got here we had enough to eat up a keep good heart dear wife and remember that god has spared me this time and to him we must look for the future so here is a kiss for you give my love to all Direct your letter to Carver hospitile Washington D C Ward 76 John F Austin

Letter XXIV. *With it being judged that his wounds were not mortal, Austin and many other wounded Rhode Islanders were removed to Portsmouth Grove Hospital, located several miles north of Newport, Rhode Island. The hospital was well maintained and many of the men enjoyed good care. It was here that John and Emily were finally reunited. She would make weekly visits from Ashland to visit John at Portsmouth Grove, while Austin continued to write her letters.*

Portsmouth Jan 22 1863

Dear
Wife i now take my pen in hand to let you now how i am gitting along i kepe along about the same i cannot see that i git any better my back keeps lame yet and i cough a good deal nights and i have not a good apitite yet i got your letter dated the 20 and was glad to heare that you was all well at home they will not give any passes now on the account of the smallpox but there is not any body got it in the ward where i am and they say that they cannot discharg any more till they see if it spreads any more there is only 3 got it

now and they are out side of the lines and if it does not spread more it will not last long you wanted to now why they moved me it was to get them that is sick and to git them moved around in wards togeather i am as comfortable as i was in the other place only this ward is not plastered but i do not see but it is as warm as the other you wanted to know if any of the folks form the citiy had come down there they have not any of them been down here yet but old Ely wrote me a letter and he wrote that they send the letter of Dr. Arnold[25] by Mr Luther C Warner and he wrote that he would help me to git my discharge but i do not know how they came by Dr. Arnold letter i want you to write wheter he sent it by mail or not i do not want to git home except by pass or anything else now or at least not till they see how them cases of small pox comes as they do not think much about it heare and i think that when you git ready you had better come and see me again and tell your mother and all the rest to come if they can i cannot think of anything more to write at present give my love to all the folks and tell them that i should like to see them all so i must bring my letter to a close so Emily heare is a kiss for you

    from your husband

    John F Austin

Letter XXV. *Emily Austin continued to visit John at the hospital. She made a nuisance of herself pleading with the doctors to let Austin return to Scituate. A small pox scare led the hospital to ban all visitors, while the disease was contained. Austin soon developed complications from his head wounds and found himself with severe back and heart problems.*

---

[25] A surgeon at Portsmouth Grove Hospital.

Portsmouth Grove Feb 8 1863

Dear
  Wife i now take my pen in hand to answer your letter which i receved saturaday and was well glad to heare that you was all well at home except yourself i am afraid that you have exposed yourself to much for me trying to do something for me and i want you to be careful and not git sick for the doctor says that you cannot hurry my discharge and that i will be examined when my turn comes but this morning the doctor that doctors in my ward when he came around to me and felt my puls and then examined my stomach and i think that he thought that i had some disease of the heart for he sent out to another doctor and he came in and examined me then they went in the stewards room and talked a while but i do not no what they call it but they gave me three drops of something and told me the nurse to be shure and not giv any more if he did to pour it our and wash the spoon[26] and give me more if need be so i think there is something the matter with my heart my back is about the same as it was when you was there it does not seem to got any better yet you said that i might think it strang that you did not till i got your lettr and then i thought it was the best thing that you could do to get back hime as you could do nothing for me and you would have to go right to newport and stay all night then back in the morning and i think it better for you not to come till there is a place for you to stay all night with the farmer but there is sine more cases of the veraloid but i do not think much about that and i think that albert and the boys better wait a while and i can write to you when to come not but what I am ankcious to see you all but

---

[26] Civil War doctors experimented with many different medicines on their patients, some of which they knew not what they were. Whiskey was often the prescribed medicine for all types of illness and wounds.

you cannot git a place to stay unless you go to newport and that will cost you to much for i think that it will not be long before you can stay an around heare somewhere give my love to all the folks and tell them i should like to see them all and that i hope i shall before long Emily i cannot fill up this sheet as my hand is rather week so i shall have to bring this letter to a close by sending you a good kiss i should like to have two dollars if you have it to spare write as soon as you git this so good bye for the time

From your husband
John F Austin

Letter XXVI.

Portsmouth Grove Feb the 27th 1863
Dear Wife i now take my pen in hand to let you now how i am gitting along and to answer your letter which i recived to day i am about the same as i was my back pains me so that i have to sit up all nights and sleep some of the time and i have the palpation of the heart so that if i lay on my back it chooks me up so i must be up nights most of the time i got your letter and the money and i hope that i shall not have to send for any more for i hope that i shall git home next week i think that you had better not come tll next monday as they are going to muster in for pay this week and i asked the doctor about the small pox and he says that there is not a case of it on the ground now and if it does not break out again that they are a going to begin to send them off next week and that he thinks that we will git an examination pretty soon but i want you to come down next week you and Josiah as quick as it is good weather and see me the doctors says that the quarentine will be off next week if the small pox does not break out again Emily somtimes i git discourages and think that i do not care whether i live or not and then again i think if i can only live to see my mother and

take care of her for i know that she and my dear wide is worrying about me all the time and i shall be thankful to him who lives above and there is many others that often run through my mind that i should like to see again tell my mother that if i can i will soon come and see her once more and have that kind care of a mother and wide again give my love to all the folks and tell them that i should like to see them all Emily here is a kiss for you on paper but i hope soon to have on from thy face so good night

From your husband
John F Austin

Letter XXVII. John F. Austin's wounds were judged by Doctor Francis L. Wheaton to be too severe to permit him to return to the Seventh Rhode Island. As such he was given a medical discharge on March 14, 1863 and returned to Ashland several days later.

US Hospital Portsmouth Grove March the 11th 1863

Dear
    Wife i now take my pen in hand to let you now how i am gitting along i am about the same as ususual and hope these few lines will find you the same i suppose that you are looking for me home every day now i think if nothing happens that i shall ne up Thursday or Friday the doctor has promised to examin us to day and i hope if i get my discharge that i shall be up tomorrow or next day i want you to stay there this week and i hope i shall git up there this week if not i want you to be shure and come down next week but the doctor say that he is going to git me off as quick as he can so do not he discouraged for i think as quick as he can so do not be discouraged for i think that i will be at home before long wher we shall not be separated again very soon i had a

letter from pardon yesterday and he wrote that he was going home Saturday and that he was well and doing well and i am glad to heare that so i will not write any more at present so heare is another kiss for you Emily From your Husband
John F Austin

Corporal John F. Austin returned to Ashland and his job at the Ashland Manufacturing Company. He would die in 1886, still suffering from the effects of his wounds.

CHAPTER THREE

Private Abel B. Kenyon

Abel B. Kenyon was a twenty-five year old farmer from Hopkinton. He enlisted in the Seventh on August 25, 1862, along with his brother in laws Joseph Weeden Burdick and Isaac N. Saunders. Kenyon was married to Burdick's sister Julia and lived upon his father in law's farm. Despite enlisting in Company A with his relatives, Kenyon found himself in Company K. Company A recruited above its full complement of men and several were required to transfer to Company K to fill this company to its required strength. Kenyon wrote this very vivid letter a week after the Battle of Fredericksburg, describing his experiences there. This letter is one of the best descriptions of the Seventh's charge. It reveals the fear of a soldier that after surviving one horrible battle, that he would soon be forced into another.

Camp near Frederick Burg, Va. Dec 26. 1862

Brother Benjamin,
      I received your letter last night and was glad to hear from you though you did not say in particular whether you were all sick or well. I take it that you are all well at least I hope so we boys are all well as usuall and I feel verry thankful for it you spoke of the 7 Reg being in the Battle I think it was and in a warm one we marched over the river six day morning and lay around in the streat that day and night & seaventh day morning the shells bursted closte

to us one bursted within 12 feet of me & killed one man & wounded another[27] you had better believe that the boys began to look around themselves we stood that until about noon then we started for the field there was nothing said but a good deal of thinking if rest was like me I can tell you that the canon balls and rifle ballls come thick and fast when we was going on to the field but we went up in good line though we had to walk over many dead and wounded men we loded our pieces on our knees and lying down I rose and fired and layed down again we was in line on the field about five hours until after dark the rifle balls sounded just like a swarm of bees huming around the hive we marched off the field back to the citty about ½ mile into the old building any where we could for the night our Col. Bliss said to us he did not feel like making a speech but he would say to us we had the honor of doing the best of any Regiment on the field it was a sad time any way we can fix it such a time I never want to see again but verry likely we shall see more fighting if we do I hope the Lord will be with us and carry us safe through & be permitted to return home once more and see you all again I dont want you to send them boots until we send for them tell Julia I want a vest made something cheap that will be warm I have not time nor paper to rite more so I will close by sending my respecks to you all write soon

Abel B. Kenyon

I would like to have a little money they have not paid us off yet and dont know as they ever will I want Government money if you have any let Julia see this and the old folks I havent got any paper to write her as soon as I can get some I will write. Yours ever A.B.K.

---

[27] This man is Private Henry S. Cole of Foster, his remains were never recovered.

In the years of war ahead, Kenyon would again see the unspeakable scenes of battle. His brother in law, Joseph Weeden Burdick would die of Yazoo Fever in Mississippi. His other brother in law, Isaac N. Saunders was killed in action at Spotsylvania. Kenyon himself would be wounded in the head at Jackson, Mississippi and in the hand at Spotsylvania. Abel B. Kenyon was mustered out on June 9, 1865. He returned to Julia and his farm in Hopkinton.

CHAPTER FOUR

Corporal Charles P. Nye

Charles P. Nye was a laborer from Richmond when he enlisted in the Seventh. Like Abel B. Kenyon, and ten other men from Richmond and Hopkinton, Nye was assigned to Company K. He still maintained close connections to his friends in Company A. These letters were written to Benjamin Pendleton of Richmond. Pendleton also maintained correspondence with several other men in the Seventh Rhode Island.

Letter I. *Nye wrote this letter as the Seventh arrived at the Army of the Potomac encampment at Pleasant Valley, Maryland waiting while the Army commanders decided to make their next move.*

Pleasant Valley MD Oct 8-1862

Friend Benjamin

I take this oppurtunity to write you a few lines to lit no how I am a getting along I am well as I ever was in my life we are encamped the tavern two mountain sides the Rebels come through bout two weeks ago the 4th RI Regt as camped about ¾ of a mile from us and all of Burnside army is camped round now I have had some good time since I have been out here we was camped in Fredrick City about a week ago and their was a lot of prety Girls I was telling em we did not drill any in two days and I crused around the city

hundred mils last week but have got ther a riding and hard got the foot I expect not to write any more becase got three others send me more peper. Give my best respects to Amy, Abby, and the girls I must go write to me how the folks are a getting along and all the particlars
    Direct to
        Charles P. Nye
        Co K 7th Regt R.I.V.
        Washington   DC.

Letter II. *The Seventh remained in Pleasant Valley, as Ambrose Burnside took command of the Army of the Potomac. Disease continued to persist in the Seventh, starting with an outbreak of typhoid in Company A.*

                      Pleasant Valley MD. Oct 22/62

Friend Benjamin
        I take my pen and hand to inform you that I received your letter last night and was glad to hear from you and the rest of the folks. and I am Glad to hear that they are haveing meeting and I hope it will be to the benefit of all that attend them and that the church will take more intrest in them then the dud some when I was there. I am well at present and enjoy myself verry well I have gaind eight lb since I have come out here. some of the boys say thay they do not have enough to eat I can not say so for if you could see my haversack you would say I would not starve. I expect your have hear that George

Corporal Charles P. Nye

Gardiner and Frank Collins[28] is dead they was buried day before yesterday the funeral was preached by our Chaplain and a prayer was made by Let Marton[29] the 9th New Hampshire Brass Band Led the prosesion to the grave followed by our drum band and thin eighteen of Company A with reverse arms then the cops and then the rest of com. A, than came the whole Regiment with commissioned Officers in the rear the text was taken in the 5 chapter if Ja Cob 60 verse after the cops was then lowered in to their graves three vollys was fired over their grave and then we returned to our quarters. it was the Solomens sene that I ever witness John Lewis and Thomas Briggs[30] are sick but they are so that they

---

[28] Both men were from Company A and resided in Hopkinton. They were the first of many men to die in the Seventh of typhoid fever. Gardner died on October 19, and Collins died on October 18.

[29] Unidentified.

[30] John D. Lewis of Hopkinton died of typhoid fever at Falmouth, Virginia on December 25, 1862. Thomas B. Briggs of West Greenwich

go out doors the rest of the boys are well as far as I know. I do not know of any more new to write for you hear all of the news before we do here Give my respects to the Girls and tell Sarah + Card that I have got off now where she can not break any pipes fore me now and where I am see no girls to hug Black or White-Give my best respect to all and write-as soon as conveniant Direct as before

Yours Charles P. Nye

Letter III. *Following the Battle of Fredericksburg, the Seventh returned to its camp at Falmouth and again suffered terribly from disease. With many men ill and some still recovering from their wounds suffered at Fredericksburg. The regimental surgeons were kept occupied in their duties and many of the men in the Seventh received their discharges and were sent home; many to die of the disease contracted in the service.*

Camp near Falmouth Va Feb/2.63

Friend Benjamin

I recevied your letter saturday and was glad to hear that you well I am enjoying good health at present and I hope when these few lines reaches you they will find you and your enjoying the same blesing. We have had some very Disagreable weather here for the last fortnite the mud here is two and three feet deep in some places now we had a tedous snow stom here last wendnesday the snow fell about six inches deep [we had to go on Picket in at down besides the river without tents.] Our Regiment came out with nine hundred and sixty four men and when we was called out to go on Picket we could not Muster but two hundred and eight three men we can not muster over four hundred cook teamers

---

spent much of his time in the service working at the draft camps near New Haven, Connecticut. He would be mustered out with the regiment.

and all fit for duty. most of the boys are well that came from around your way tell Mrs Lewis that I do not think she would know George Henry[31] he is so fat GN Richmond is well and gets along much better then I thought he would when I heard that he had enlisted I have heard several times that Wealthy Lamphere[32] has got a bushy if so I wish you would write who it belongs to the boys plaugue Has and Potter and tell him that it belong to him and he says it belongs to John I His Cox[33] I now of no news to write but when you have heard give best respects to all inquring friends and write as soon as conveniant write all of the particlars especially about the young folks I must close and get my dinner. I dont think I shall need a women by the time I get home am going to set up a "Batchlors Hall" if I ever live to get home I remain Your Lucid Friend

Charles P. Nye

Letter IV. *Following the disastrous "Mud March," Burnside resigned his command of the Army of the Potomac. He then regained command of his Ninth Corps. In mid-February the Ninth Corps was sent to Newport News, Virginia to await orders. Many men felt as though they were being banished for having Burnside as their corps commander. They waited here until orders were received in the middle of March directing the regiment to Lexington, Kentucky. From here, the Seventh participated in the Mississippi Campaign.*

---

[31] George Henry Lewis was a resident of Hopkinton and a private in Company A. He survived the entire war without being injured.
[32] The Lamphere's were a wealthy family in Hopkinton at this time and owned several textile mills.
[33] John T. Hiscox of Company A, also a resident of Hopkinton. He was wounded at Bethesda Church and was mustered out on June 9, 1865.

Newport New. Va. March 7/63

Friend Benjamin
	Your letter of the 1st came duly at hand and I hasten to write you a few lines to let you know that I am well and was Glad to hear from you and the rest of the folks. and to hear that they were all enjoying good health We are now on the best camp ground that we have ever been on since we left Camp Bliss RI now how long are shall stay here I do not know it is rumoed that Burside is to take commant and take us farther south but how true it is I do not know some of the boys here are sick with the Meales George Henry Lewis George Langworthy jine J. Weaden Burdick are in the Hospital sick with them now Burr Clark is just getting over with them Horace Slocum[34] is in the Hospital sick and he is in bad shape too and I do not think he will ever get well if he stays here Horace Potter[35] is pretty tickeled to think that he has got clear of that scrape. I do not know of any news to write but what you have heard I am olny 29 lbs Heaver than I was when I left Rhode Island Soldiering agrees with me first rate Give my best respects to all of the folks especially the Girls tell them that I expect to coome home and see some of them when this war ends Write as soon as you can
		I remain your most
			Lucid Friend
			Charles P. Nye

---

[34] All of these men were in Company A. George W. Langworthy was a resident of Ashaway. He was wounded on April 2, 1865. He would later found the first library in his town. Joseph Weeden Burdick was also from Hopkinton. He would die at Milldale, Mississippi on July 19, 1863 of Yazoo Fever. John Burr Clark was a resident of Richmond. He was severely wounded at Fredericksburg and would die of the measles on May 10, 1863 at Baltimore, Maryland. Horace Slocum also resided in Richmond; he was wounded at Fredericksburg and would survive the war.
[35] Horace Potter is unidentified, but he was not a soldier.

Benjamin W. Pendleton

Letter V. *Following the Mississippi Campaign, the Seventh returned to Lexington, Kentucky in a well worn condition. They could barely muster one hundred and fifty men. Nearly fifty Rhode Islanders would lose their lives to the disease they suffered in Mississippi and almost a hundred more were sick in the hospitals of Cincinnati, Ohio.*

Tuesday August 25th 1863
Friend Benjamin
I take these few leasure momets to write to you to let you know that I am alive and well. I recevied a letter from you last 4th of July but as we had to march on Jackson and have been moovin round so I have not had time to write or do hardly any thing before we are now back in Old Kentucky once more where the people are not fraid of us and run when they hear that the Yankees are coming and tell their Negroes that we will kill them if do not keep out of our way. Our Regt. marched about two hundred miles in Mississippi and was in the fight twenty four hours at Jackson. we lost but two killed and 12 wounded, and 6 prisoners at Jackson and 12 has died of sickness[36] since we were in Mississippi and on River but I have been lucky. I have been well through all of the trip. I do not know of any news but what you have heard Give my best respects to the girls and write as often as you can and I will try to do better next time. Pardon Wright[37] has got back to the Regiment and he looks as rugged as a bear.

I remain Yours
With respect
Charles P. Nye

Letter VI. *Upon returning to Kentucky in a much worn out condition, the Seventh became the provost guard of the town. The people were in general friendly to the men, but they would occasionally face Confederate guerillas under John Hunt Morgan.*

---

[36] Nye's casualty figures are very correct for the time. However many more Rhode Islanders would die from the disease they would face in Mississippi.
[37] Pardon T. Wright of Company A.

Charles P. Nye

Nicholes Ville Ky.

Sept. 21th 1863

Friend Benjamin
I received your letter yesterday and I was glad to hear that you and your family was well. I am well at present and as fat as a hog I weigh one hundred and fifty four pounds thirty pounds more than I weigh when I came from Mississippi for that trip came hard on me but I did not have to cuse in but I thought I should several time. I heard that Henry Godfrey[38] was dead the last time I saw him was coming up the Mss River and he looked verry feble but I hoped that by the change of climat it would cure him but it went the other way I am sorry for his folks they must feal bad. The Regiment is at Lexington now doing Provost duty and I am on a detail a detail at Nicholas Ville doing Provost duty here we was call out this morning to go down town to see the Rebels go through that Burnside captured at Cumberlan Gap and see that more of them held any conversation with any of the Citizens here. there was about a dozen of them belong in this place. They was the hard lot of looking men that I ever saw they looked so that they ought to have a good scrubbing with soop and watter thet was dressed in all colours and all shapes. I do not know of any now to write at present

please write soon and direct to

Charles P. Nye
Nicholasville
Ky.
Yours with Respects

Corp. Charles P. Nye

---

[38] Henry Godfrey was from Hopkinton. He was discharged July 27, 1863 after suffering from Yazoo Fever, but died a month later in Rhode Island.

Letter VII. *After again suffering heavy losses in the Overland Campaign of 1864, the Seventh garrisoned the forts around Petersburg, Virginia. Corporal Nye was slightly wounded on July 8, at Petersburg. At this time, the regiment moved to the aptly named Fort Hell. Fort Sedgewick, as it was formally named was the closest fort to the Confederate defenses. Injury was a constant threat at Fort Hell. Most of the time, many of the men lived in underground shelters called "bombproofs."*

Camp 7th Regt RI Vols
Fort Sedgewick Jan 15th 1865

Friend Benjamin
          Not hearing from you in some time I thought that I would pen you a few lines to let you know that I am still among the living and enjoying good health We are camp in a Fort called Fort Hell by the Soldiers and dit is the roughest hole that I ever got in to we have to live in holes made in the ground to keep out of the way of the Jonnies mess kitlles and boot legs which they throw over occasionaly doing but little damage to our Regiment-as yet- Our Picket lines are so close together in some pleasces that they can throw crackers over at each other. They do not shoot any in the day but in the night they make the balls whistle around there. Our Regiment is not doing Picket Duty now but we have to go out in the woods evry other day and make a gabion a peice I suppose you would like to know what a gabion is it is made like a basket only there is no Bottom. They are three feet high and eighteen inches wide.[39] I would like to be at home a little while to see how things are getting

---

[39] After being reduced to only a hundred effectives by July of 1864, the Seventh was pulled off the line and acted as engineers for the Second Division, Ninth Corps.

along I have got about eight more months to serve for Uncle Sam then if they get me again they have got to be Smarter than I am. I hope the thing will taley out soon. I do not Know of any more news to write If you have time I would like to have you write how the young folks are getting alon.

    I Remain Your With Respect

    Direct to Charles P. Nye
        Co K 7th Regt R.I.V.
        Washington
            D.C.

Letter VIII. *The Seventh remained at Fort Hell, and heard the news that Sherman had advanced from Savannah on his way to Charlestown, South Carolina.*

    Fort Hell Va. Feb 6th 1865
    Friend Benjamin
        Your of the 30th came in hand this morning it found me in good health and good spirits I hope that this will find you and your famlie in good health All of the troops have mooved to the left except just enough to hold the front line and our Regiment happened to be one of the luck one to stop back the last raid that they made we had a hard time but we will look ate the Jonnies while they fight them this time I hear Sherman is in Command of this Raid I hope that he will come out all right. I do not know where they have gone Our boys are on the very good terms with the Rebs here you can hear them talking to gather near half of the time When we first come here they was shooting half of the time so It was not safe to go around much I suppose that you have heard all

of the [news] of any interest. G H Potter[40] and George Lewis and George Langworthy are well and sends thier respects to you. Give my Respects to all enquiring firends Write soon

remain yours
With Respect
Charles P. Nye
Co K 7th Regt RIV
Washington DC

Letter IX. *The Seventh remained at Fort Hell until April 2, when they stormed into Petersburg. One week later, Lee would surrender at Appomattox Court House.*

Camp of 7th Regt RI Vols
Fort Hell March 2nd 1865

Friend Benjamin

Yours of the 26th came at hand this morning and as it has been rainnning to day it made it so dark in here I could not write with out a candle. I am well and I hope that this will find you and yours the same. we have had some verry fine weather here for the last month but this month has come in cold and rinny but how long it will last I do not know I hope not for long for I do not like wet weather without cover on gurd and picket but I suppose we shall have to take it as it comes for the next six months as we had the last thirty. I hear that Ed has got into a scrape with Sisson Carpenter I want you write all about it for I want to know about it the boys are all well do not think of any news to write time my love to all to ant Abby and the rest of the folks write and add the partuclars

I remain yours with respects

---

[40] George H. Potter of Foster and Richmond would be wounded at Fredericksburg and Bethesda Church. Potter would end the war as a sergeant in Company K.

Charles P. Nye
Co K 7th RIV
Washington D.C

Letter X. *With the surrender of the Army of Northern Virginia at Appomattox, the Seventh returned to Washington D.C. and prepared for the Grand Review of the United States Armies. One night, several men in the regiment lit candles on the ends of their muskets and paraded through the company streets. In turn it spread to the entire regiment and soon the entire army was parading that night.*

Camp of 7th Regt R.I Vols
near Alexandia May 18th

Friend Benjamin
    Yours of the 14th came at hand last night it found me in good health and enjoying myself as well as can be for a Soldier. I was sorry to hear that John Bigg[41] was dead. I suppose that things will look odd to me when I get home being away so long. We are camped on a nice place here where we can view the old Potomac we had one of the nicest sights here about a week ago. two Divisions of our corps exhuminated all of their tents and then they all fell into lines with a light apeard about twenty thousand of them it was one of the finest sights that I ever saw it all started from our Regiment I see by the morning paper that a grand review of all of the armes is coming off tuesday and Wednesday I shall be glad when it all comes off for we will stand some sight to get home I hate a review worse then any thing in soldiering but we have to take things as they come. the Boys are all well George Lewis is down guarding paroled

---

[41] John Briggs was a resident of Smithfield. He was discharged as a minor before the Seventh had even left Rhode Island. He died in 1865, having never served in the army.

prisoniers but will be relieved this morning I must close excuse poor writing give my Respects to all and write soon

From your Friend
Charles P Nye
Co K 7th Regt RIV
Washington
DC

Charles P. Nye returned to Rhode Island and spent his remaining years in Richmond.

CHAPTER FIVE

Sergeant Charles F. Colvin

Sergeant Charles Frank Colvin was born in South Scituate on April 4, 1836. He was a farmer and worked upon his grandfather's farm. He married Maria Handy in 1860 and had five children. Colvin enlisted in Company K on August 8, 1862 to serve for three years. He wrote these letters to his brother Oliver Colvin, whom lived with him upon his farm.

Letter I. *At this time the Seventh had been had their camp at Pleasant Valley for several weeks, waiting while the Army of the Potomac made their next move. It was here that an outbreak of typhoid hit Company A.*

Pleasant Valley
Maryland Oct 22 1862

Dear Brother
I received your letter the 21 and was very glad to here from you now that you was giting well again you must bee carefull of your helth or Russel Matterson will whip you I herd you and he cum pretty near fighting the other day I hav herd of your quiriling with him five times if I hear of it once more I shal beleav you did thare was three men dide in co A thare was two of them buried Monday at once that is all of the thing that I have seen since I left home that made me feel lonesome thare was 700 went to the grave the Brass band went and it plade the lonesome tune that ever hird then

thay fied three rounds over them I tell you that maid me field lonesome thare are a good menny sick in the Regt at presant thare is diferent kinds of sickness but the mane sickness is homesickness and one more kind of complant that thay brought with them I tell you it givs them hell laying on the ground and eating baken I hav had the best helth since I left home that I hav had in three years if I can keep so I ask no odds of the rebile I can stay with them a while yet
thare was some of the boys left the 7th RI Regt and went and Eddy went joined the battery and was in the last battle thar was some of them wonded and one kiled so thay say I dont now enny one of them the battle was mos near anuf to us so we herd the cannons[42] planeas day Stephen A. Harrington[43] is verry much out of helth he has ben off duty two week he is week and has a very lame back we are under marching orders now we are liable to go enny one I cant think of enny more at presant I am boiling beans now and I leav of or thay will burn tell Charly thatI should like to hav him right a line or two to me dont tell noboddy that I put harrington name in this for it makes him mad Eddy Perce[44] rote that he was sick and he was mad said he could do his own righting I found this out since I begun this dont share it tell Arvilly that it wantsa harder hart thah she has got if

---

[42] "Eddy" is Private John Eddy of Glocester. He later died of disease contracted in the service. The battery they joined was Battery D, First Rhode Island Light Artillery. Battery D was recruited in northwestern Rhode Island and contained a large proportion of men from Foster and Scituate. Heavily engaged at Antietam, the unit lost twenty men fighting in Miller's Cornfield. It drafted men from the infantry regiments around it to replace the artillerists.

[43] Sergeant Stephen A. Harrington a fellow soldier from Scituate in Company K. Harrington was sick for the greater part of his service, including the period described by Colvin. He died April 6, 1889.

[44] Edwin O. Pierce of Scituate enlisted with his fellow Scituate comrades in Company K. Like many other soldiers he was unable to stand the rigors of the campaign and was transferred to the Veterans Reserve Corps in 1865. He was mustered out on July 13, 1865.

Sergeant Charles F. Colvin

not every friday would run ove them that sufr in the hard is the best felow tell my folks I am well

Charles F. Colvin

Letter II. *Following the Battle of Fredericksburg the Seventh spent a miserable winter encampment near Falmouth, Virginia. Here outbreaks of dysentery, typhoid, and pneumonia would plague the Seventh.*

Camp Opersit of Fredrick Burg Citty Near falmoth
January the 18 1863

Dear Brother
I now take my pen in hand to inform you that I am as well as comon and hope these few lines will find you the same thare

has not been nothing worth riting of about we are still at the same place we are under marching orders and hav been most of the time for the 2 last weeks but dont no where we are going some think we are going in to a nother battle some think we are going back for better quarters but thare is no noing whire we are going thare is a good menny sick ones hear and growing more and more every day thare is every day from 3 to 8 buried every day Thos Remengton[45] told me yesterday that we was losing 3 a day on the average and of the 7 we hav left some back long and some dyes and some gits thare discharege and all together makes 3 a day regles out of the 7 RI Regt and them that is reported for duty is down harted and dis satisfid thay hant payed us and that makes the boys mad thay hav partly paid the 4 RI they ode them 6 months and payed them for 4 and took out pay for the first suit of close that was found by the state and all of the solgers exspected that suit was giv to them and now thay charge 27.50 for them and thay had drawn some Clothing all together made 36 and some more one man ode the government 3 thare was sum men that did not git much Bounty[46] and thare family is sufering for the want of the money and if thay do so by me I shal cum home or dy trying the boys from the way is well as comon but Ben F Serls[47] he is rather down at presant Denis is A bout the same Harry is A bout the same the 4 RI say thay never will fite more for nothing but the cused nigers if thay had paid them and was

---

[45] Thomas J. Remington served as a private in Company B of the Seventh.

[46] Many towns in Rhode Island offered large bounties to join the Seventh Rhode Island. In Foster and Scituate the bounty was four hundred dollars. In addition the Rhode Island troops would experience similar problems in the years following the war as they fought to receive their pensions for their services, but they were curtailed as they had been charged for two sets of uniforms.

[47] Benjamin F. Searles of Cranston. He was discharged on account of illness on December 30, 1863.

trying bes to the men thay would go in but thay did not come hear to bee punished to free the niges I dont think of enny more at presant tell Nathan and Charly I should like to hear a word from them I want them to rite a little if it is nothing more than Kiss my Ass

This is all this time so good by this is from your Brother
Charles F. Colvin
Rite soon
Without
Complant

Letter III. *After contracting typhoid fever, Colvin was transferred to the Portsmouth Grove Hospital to recover from his illness. On June 7, 1864 he rejoined the Seventh and was assigned to the pioneer corps; soldiers who built roads and fortifications.*

Portmouth Grove hospittle Ward 21 December the 19 1863

Dear Brother I now take my pen
in hand to in form you that I am A little better than I was but I tremble pretty bad now and my back plages me yet I dont take no medess on now all I hav to do so far is to make my one bed and eat and that hant but A damed little work for we don't hav much to eat we don't fair half so swell as we did with the Regt when we was in camp I think R.I. keeps fine hospittle we hav a little soup for dinner 2 or 3 potatoes for supper and a little salt and A small peas of white bread with it A little Rice or mush and molasses
for brakefast that cold and not half enuf thare is over 900 hear now thare is a good menny of the 7 RI thare was three boys left out of ward No 5 last night thay hant back yet one

was Denis Galegy[48] of River point I think he will go home the other two I dont no thare names one said he was going to go to newport the other was going to providence with Galegy mebby thay will come back and not go I dont want you to tell that I roat to you a bout them if thay should find out that I did thay would kill me they will bee reported derectly if they arnt back in 48 ours we hav 4 good big bedrooms thare is 56 beds in it now thay took out 20 this fall the bedstids are all iron the fethers are irish such as corn leaves and rye-straw it seem like hell to day Thay tell about having a good time to Porthmouth grove hospittle and what good fais they hav thare the next man that I hear tell that I will knock him down the ward rules is a damd sightcloster and stricter than thay was to the Regt thare was a inspection yesterday and another to morrow to see who would do for thare Regt and who would do for the first Batalion and who would do for the second Batalion I dont know wether thay will send me to my Regt or what thay will do thaydont say much to me whether I am better or wors the boys think thay will put me in to the secont Battalion I think thay will send me to the Regt I came I cant think of no more at present give my love to mother and all the rest so good bye this is from your

Brother Charles F. Colvin rite soon

Direct your letters
Sergt. Charles F. Colvin
Porthmouth Grove
Hospittle Ward No. 21

Letter IV. *Incomplete. The first page of this letter is missing from the collection and no proper background information can be given to it.*

---

[48] Unidentified.

Give my love to Freelove and Charly and Nathan tell mother that I hate to dispute his word but if I ever git out of this I show him the diference he had better in gay his custimers for I may giv him a flop before he thinks of it I want Charley to rite to me if he knows whire Henry Capesin is he belongs to East Greenwitch and he scedadled from Fredrick the time of the Battle and thay hav told that thay cetched him and I want to no tell Charly to tell his womon that She must look out or we will hon him out hear se how goes the boys talk a bout the war that has got home do they like it tell Stephen A Harington and Henry Pears that thay did not cum out further nuf to no whether thay liked it or not I dont wish them no hurt but I wish thay had gorn once to Fredrick hights with us I had a letter today from Ruth thay are all as well as comon the Sight is good for plenty of fighting and if enny If you want to fight com Out and try it
Rite Soon I am good for the Nigger War
If you want to fight com
Out and try it
Rite Soon
I am good for the Nigger War Yet

Letter V. *Following their participation in the Grand Review, the Seventh prepared to be mustered out of service. Here the Seventh was mustered out on June 9, 1865. In addition the men of the Seventh first began to experience problems that would plague them for many years after the war. They received two sets of uniforms, those by the state, and the Federal government. The government however charged the soldiers for their uniforms issued by the state. This would lead to sharp battles after the war for their pensions.*

7 Regt RI Co K Camp Nere Alexandria VA June 1865

Dear Brother I now take my pen to in form you that I am well and all right and hope these few lines will find you the same I receved your kind letter last night and was glad to here from you I gues evry thing is agoing all right the government is agoing to take $27 ½ for the state suit which thay was to giv me and if maria has given away the children and sold my things I am in a bout the same fix the rebs is cleaned up but a Soldger never frets I don't want her to sell my things nor give away my things I exspect to appere in RI in Side of 2 weeks and if I can help my Self I will if I cant let it go I shant loos no Sleep I guess She is missing It I dident think of this but It is hard telling what will happne in war times giv my love to all the folks this is all I hav time to rite so good bye
This is from your Brother

CF Colvin

Sergeant Charles F. Colvin was mustered out on June 9, 1865. Following the war he became a laborer in Scituate. He died of paralysis on November 19, 1879 while engaged in his work.

CHAPTER SIX

Private William H. Jordan

William H. Jordan resided in the village of Harris in Coventry and was a clerk in a Hope, Rhode Island mill before the war. He enlisted in Coventry on August 11, 1862 to serve for three years in the Seventh. When this letter was written, the Seventh had just completed a march in the middle of winter to eastern Kentucky with scant provisions and poor clothing; no men died but several suffered from frost bite.

> Camp 7th R I Vol
> Point Isabella Ky
> Jan 11th 64

Dear Brother Sister & Feriends
I seat my self
to write you a few lines to let you know that I am yet upon the land of the living and ma well and hope this will bing you all injoying the same great blessing. you have no doubt herd of our moove ment from Lexington and we have had a tought time in getting here I cannot describe the journey to you better then for you to imagin a Regt of men marchig through RI in the very worst of weather in the winter through the roughfest of the country but there is no country in RI 1/100 part as bad with nothing but shelter tents scrapeing off the snow and ice to find a place to lie down that is the best description I can give for such it is a has binn. new years day was as cold a dy. I think as I bout ever see it was so cold that

Colonel Zenas R. Bliss

we did not march that day we kept good fires there were plenty of fence but I never had so hard work to keep warm in my life I don't know as I frose me any where unless I did one of my heels that is some sore Some of the boys froze their limbs George Becford[49] froze his ears stiff I felt them and they were froze hard as a stick we are going to stay here some time I gess Col. Bliss comands the post here and they are buiding winter quarters for us as fast as they can it is verry Mount ainous country out here there is going to be a military post here they are buiding now, there is not but one or two houses here we are camped on a hill in the woods. I have binn down to help take up the Genstone bridge to da the river was all frose over one man said he had lived here for 30 years and never see the river froze over before

Ben said in your last letter jen wanted me to name your babe but I expect you have named it before now but if you are wateing for me to name it you may call it

Selinda Mannery

that is the best name I can think of it is if jen dont like it name it something els I must close for the present good bye

Yours with respect
Wm H. Jordan

After surviving the campaigns of 1864 Private Jordan was detailed as a clerk in the United States Quartermaster Department in January 1865, he held this position until June 9, 1865 when he was mustered out of the service. William H. Jordan returned to Coventry and continued to work in the mills.

---

[49] George C. Beckford was an immigrant from England. He served three years as a private in Company D.

CHAPTER SEVEN

Private William O. Harrington

Private William O. Harrington was a thirty-two year old apple and dairy farmer whom resided in the village of Moosup Valley, located in southern Foster. He enlisted in the regiment on August 11, 1862. He left behind his wife, Eunice and his children; Ida and Edwin. A third child, William was born shortly after he left the state, and would not be named for several months. His letters are unique in this set as they span the entire history of Company K. Harrington was never injured or sick during his service. He is of no relation to Sergeant William Harrington of Company D, whom died of disease in Kentucky in 1863.

Letter I. *Following their departure from Providence on September 10, 1862 the Seventh proceeded in a multi-stage journey to Washington. Along the way Harrington would meet his brother, First Lieutenant Josiah Harrington.*

Washington DC Sept 13

My dear wife
This morning I find myself in the capitall after three days journeying we started from camp Bliss on wednesday noon + marched to Marsh bay depot 2 ½ miles arrived at Groton at 10 we started for Ny arrived in york at 6 and started for south Amboy new Jersey at 10 arrived threre at 5 pm changed from steamboat to cars and started rite for philidelphia and got our supper which was furnished by the

sitty folks in good style after supper we start for Baltimore and rode all night and got to Baltimore about 10 oclock on the cars from philidelphia to Baltimore I saw Josiah[50] and had quite a talk with him he is stationed at a place called degrass 36 miles north of Baltimore he says his health is pretty good we started from Baltimore at 4 oclock and got to Washington at 10 oclock at night we had a good journey from Rhodes Island to Ny Ny Pen. Dela+ Maryland we saw no troops except the division that Josiah was with until we got to Balt but between there and here there is lots of them how many I don't know there is many in sight of here from the city east it looks like a hill from here and just about as far from us that is from you the entrenchments I mean I will give you more of the particulars of the citty when I write again how long we shall stay here we cant tell as we have not got settled down yet but as I wanted to here from you so I thought I would write now and let you no where to write to so that I can here from home I am well and am getting along just first rate now how do you all do and how doess the baby look and how do the children like it kiss them all for me I would like to call and see you we are in a fighting country there is a lot of slaves in camp this morning and apples I will stop for I cant tell what I have wrote read it and if you can you are lucky now take good care of your self as you can this time and direct to

      Wm O Harrington
      Co K 7 Regt R I V
      Washington DC

---

[50] First Lieutenant Josiah V. Harrington was the assistant surgeon of the 18th Connecticut; a regiment which hailed from eastern Connecticut and contained many Rhode Islanders. Harrington served throughout the war in the Shenandoah Valley and died of disease on December 1, 1864. His remains were returned to Moosup Valley and buried in the family plot at the Moosup Valley Cemetery.

Letter II.

Camp Chase Sept 26th 1862

My Dear Wife
I received your letter of the 19th last night and was very glad to here that you ware all well but do be careful and not be to smart for your health is all that you have to depend on now I am in good health and am five pounds heavier than when I left home we have to drill 4 hours a day and am injoying my self as well as a man can in a warlike country and away from home we have just come in from Brigade review there was 11 Regt on the field mustering 10,700 men and to see them all Marching some time in one solid boddy then in some other position when we start to leave the prade ground we form in line 4 abreast and it makes a long line it would surprise some of the Foster boys to see our division when in action it is ginerally believed that we shall quarter hear all winter by we [noncommisioned offissers & Boys] if we do I dont think that we shall be in a battle but as for my self I dont borrow any trouble about the futer take care of the preasant and let the futer take care of itself is my motto this war dont trouble me any more there then it did at home there is but one thing that makes me lonesome and that I the thoughts of home I should like to see you and the children and Mother the best kind I got a letter from Josiah the 21 he was well we are about 40 miles a part him he is in Baltimore there I must not write enny more at present for I must send you an order for my town bounty and a certificate that I have been in the service long enough to be entitled to my bounty so will stop I dont no what to call the baby tell what you would like to call him I gess U will send Ida that little piece tell her to be a good girl and take good care of the baby and Edwin and I will bring hime some thing pretty now good by take care of yourself and children while I come home.

From your one William

Letter III.

Plesant Vally Oct 17 1861

My Dear wife
after having indulged in the hope of getting a letter from you and no doubt sadly disappointed you I will give you a little acound of oure traviels we ware at camp chase when I last wrote Sept 27 there it was thought that we should stay there some time but the 29th we ware ordered to march to washinton and the next ordered to Frederic city we took the cars at 1 oclock and got to Fredric at 6 oclock on the morn of Oct 1 on the 3 left Fredric for Harpers Ferry got there sun down encamped withing 2 miles of the ferry we have moved 2 since and are 6 or 7 miles from the Ferry so we are in Maryland but shall cross over into V A soon we stayed here the longest that we have stayed in enny one place since we left camp chase but we have been hights favored das most of our marching as been by railroad we have seen no fighting yet but can tell you no idea of the preparation that is being made the troops agree that if they have got to fight goin and wipe out the rebellion between this and spring there is lots of Sterling and Plainfield boys in the CT 21 & 8[51] I go over to see them every few days I got a letter for Melinda last week my health is very good I have had one slight cold and that is all Mother wrote me to call the Baby but you have enny choice I had rather you would name it there I must soon fix up for review and the mail will be of

---

[51] The 21st Connecticut recruited from eastern Connecticut and several Rhode Islanders joined its ranks. Both the 8th and 21st were part of the Connecticut Brigade of the 3rd Division, Ninth Corps.

before we get back if you have wrote toell how you directed it write all the news and direct to
>
> Co K 7 Regt R I V
> Washington D C

Our tent is ful of the boys and gess that you will be bothered to make this out

Letter IV.

> Loveil Hill Oct the 31 1862

My Dere wife,
		I thought that I would write you a few lines so that you mite no where I am and that I am injoying tolerable good health not the first rate owing to having a diareah but nothing gros I have not heard form you since Oct the 5th I wrote to Mother the 24 but was oblige to stop short oing to having orders to march we have been vert buisy since then and shall likely be buisy for some time to come as there has got to be considerable fighting done within six weeks if we can rout the rebs in good shape in the next great battle which I will no doubt be fought be fore you get this as Mc Cleland and Shields[52] are on the North and west of the enemy and Burnside on the east we are with the latter and shall be held as A reserve to reinforce the tow armies unless the rebs attempt a retreat which they will not be able to do as they are in quite a force and A position between Bunkers Hill and Winchester some of our big men say we shall not see eny part of the action if they cannot be whipped without us all rite if not call us out when you write send me some stamp get fifty cents worth and send six or seven in each letter that you send then I shall be sure to get some of them I have not seen the Ct 21 for three of fore dayes although they are rite round

---

[52] Brigadier General James Shields commanded Union forces in the Shenandoah Valley.

here some where as you have not wrote annything about gittin my town bounty I think best to send you another certificate so that you can draw it I think the old order will do take good care of your self and children and live as easy as you can how is Mother and Albert how do they git along harvesting keep on account of the cost of the work so that I can tell you how much I earn myself when at home take good care of youre self and children I think that I shall be home next spring or sumer good by write soon from your William

Ps I lent my ink to george potter this fore noon thinking of writing enny more George has tented with me ever since we left R I I am his old woman now we lay beside each other nights and are very intimate and fast friends you ask Elisha if I have got to send a certificate very soon to Foster I thought that the other certificate and orders was sufficient but it seems that I have got to send one each month good by again kiss the children for me give my respects to all the folks your loving husband Wm. O. Harrington

Letter V. *After finally leaving Pleasant Valley, McClellan finally commenced a new campaign to take Richmond.*

Nov 3d 1862

Headquarters 7 Regt R I V Vol

Dear Brother
    We are now in a fighting country and we cant tell how soon we shall be called into action yesterday we made A march of 16 or 17 miles marching from 9 in the morning until 5 ½ at night it is the first long march that we have had it was quite warm yesterday all day last night it come on squaly and cold and is cold this morning we camped out in the open filds last night with orders to be ready at enny time

for action we marched all day in the driving of the cannon at Snickers gap we must be clost to that place now we are in Wilcoxs[53] army corps Gen Nagles Division all under Burnside the Bois are all in good spirits and ready to fight we hope to be victorious in the coming battels which must soon take place we all hope to git through fighting this fall so if we can go home but that is the question who will live to see spring I think that we are all in the keeping if the same god and if it is his will to spare us we shall live to see this ungodly rebellion put down my health is very good now but been rather poor so much so that I have been of from duty 10 days I have had a sever fever but have got verry well now

Nov 4 we have been out on picket duty we got along very well till 4 oclock yesterday when we ware ordered to march and we got back to camp we found that the regiment had been gone 1 ½ hours we did not find the regiment till 9 in the evening and then we ware sent forward to picket A gain we ware on the first relief so we thought to git a fine nap we had but just got to sleep when we ware routed and ordered to be in rediness to fight at anny time so we had no more sleep our company are wide A wake and in foraging for instance yesterday we got one sheep and ducks and turkeys and 3 chickens with out number we now hold the ground that a portion of the rebs held yesterday we have some 20000 troops rite round here and they say that the rebs have 35000 within three miles of here but they say that the rebs are in great free beyond the mountain but we got Mc Cleland an Shields there to deal with them all through if the enimy does not give us to much trouble on this side of the rige we shall have to cross over there to help them Colonel Bliss says we have got a buisy time for a time to come if I am wounded I will let you noit the first oppertunity I have frequently seen the Ct 21 and 8 there was no one in the 8 that I new but the

---

[53] Brigadier General Orlando B. Wilcox took over the Ninth Corps when Burnside was promoted.

Spaldin bois[54] send this to Laroy if you don't think of writing him soon if you do tell him that I am well I will write again as soon as I get through this struggle so good by for the presant Yours truly and Affectionatly

                                       Wm. O Harrington

Letter VI.

                                       Nov 17th 1862
                          Camp Near Warrington Junction

My Dear Wife
                it is with a degree of plesure that I now sit myself to write a few lines home we are now incamped about ½ miles from the Junction looking by your map you can see about where we be we are here in such force it looks a if we can conquer any force the rebbils to keep gitting back they have been falling ever since we crossed the line in to V A day before Yesterday morning we had but just left our camp where we stayed the night before when the rebbils commenced to fire on our rear gards and waggon trains doing but little damage when our artirery got to bare on them and soon stoped we had but one man wounded but the shells where falling fast around us as to my health it is good and I am enjoying myself as well as one can that is away from A happy home and all his friends our fare is plain but wholesom not mutch of a variety to be sure but enough of it we are well clothed as yet it is about time to draw some new clothes now se we shall be well clothed for the winter now dont be anny more trouble about me than you can help for you may rest asured that I shall take care of myself and trust to be at home with you and the rest of the family some time the troops seem to think the war is most over I trust it is so I

---

[54] Reuben and Charles Spaulding resided in Sterling, Connecticut and served in the 21st Connecticut Regiment.

am now going to close all thought against my will as this is now going but it is to late and so I will keep writing we have been moving most of the time and the last three weeks and allthough I have but little sundays at home we have less out here as we are as like to march sunday as any other day but we cant find fault for the smarter we move the sooner we shall git through no one can tell how glad one is to git a letter from home aspecially if it brings good news tell Mother not to think that I have forgotten or wish to slight her for not writing more particular when I write home I wrote to you all in comon I was very glad to git a letter from Mother it did me a good deal of good I have not heard from Josiah very lately and Leroy not at all so you see most of my letters come from home it is enough to if the rest dont want to write they can let it alone I write every chance I get to some one of my friends

November 20th we are encamped now at Fredricksburg where we got yesterday at one oclock after A marsh of 40 miles since I commenced this letter so you see we are quite buisy and often have to disappoint our self so well as our friends at home I think I get all the letters sent me but they are A long time coming and I often git quite out of patience waiting we are having quite a rain storm so we have to stay in our tents it is the most rain that has fallen since we left R I we anticipate staying here some days but may be ordered to march within an hour now I must close with much lov to you all I remain your William

Letter VII. *As they arrived near Falmouth, Virginia the Seventh believed they would remain there all winter and began to construct winter cabins.*

Fredric Burge Nov 24th 1862

My Dear Wife
not having any thing to doo to pass away the time and not noing when I shall have another chance to write I thought best to write and send another certificate we are still here and it is a good deal pleasanter than when I wrote before and we are gitting quite rested the mud is build up and things looks A good deal more like home you may judg how hard I fare and work when I tell you how much I weigh now 150 pounds when at home you no that I weighted 145 we draw our rations raw and cook them our selfs it would please and amuse you to come into our camp and see the different ways and means of cooking and eting the same thing we draw 1 ¼ lbs of meat 1 pound of hardbread coffee sugar beens rice[55] yesterday George and I got some meal and had a good old Johnny cake the day before we got us some chesse so we had some johnnycake and chesse we oftine talk of home and friends we have left at home we talk of sending from home a box of homemade victuals when we get into winter quarters if we live to and nothing happens if we have no fighting to do till we get to Richmond we shall be very apt to see there before we go into winter quarters it is but 50 or 60 miles frome here some think that we shall have to fight before we leave here as the rebbels are on the other side of the river our pickets oftine talk with theirs they say they are tired of the war they say that coffee is worth 3 or 4 dollars a pound sugar and salt very scarce and flower and beefe are there prinspall living with some Indian meal and salt beefe & fresh beefe for meate some time one and then the other if it could be so that I could be at home Saturday nights and Sunday with you and the children I think it would be quite a pleasant job for we have a great chance to see the country and learn the wayes of mankind if I could have my way I think there would be a great rejoicing with our troops and rebbils to for I would say

---

[55] This was the typical marching ration of the Federal soldier.

to them boyes go homeand nothing would suit them so well as to get such an order especily the old regiments I think they are ful as ancious to close the war as we are some think there is one hundred thousand troops here since I commenced this it is talked that Col Bliss has been offered the duty of garding the city this winter if we take it if that is so we shall have an easy job after it is taken I got your letter of the 12 since sundown and one from Melinda I gess you had better not attempt to send eny thing to me untill I write again which will bee soon Wm O H

Letter VIII.

VA Dec 7th 1862

My Dear Wife

With pleasure I now seat myself to write a few lines I am still injoying good health and hope to as it is one of the greatest blessings A soldier can injoy I got A letter from Jo, Malinda[56], and you last night all wrote last week was glad to hear from you all I have wrote to Sanford and Laroy boath the past week I have been over to the 21st Ct regt to see the Boise and see if them things had come they boys had not got them but thought they were at the quartermasters now I want a pair of boots and they will cost 6 ½ $ out here from home they wont cost over 4 George H Potter is going to have John O Potter[57] send him a pair and I have sent to him for a pair for me and two boxes of pills and should like to have a small cheese sent if you can afford it have John O put them in a box and direct it send them as quick as convenient and when we get paid of I will send some money to you I shall go over to see if them things come to Wm. Coal tomorrow or next day as soon as they

---

[56] Harrington's siblings consisted of Josiah, Melinda, Leroy, and Wheaton.
[57] George H. Potter's brother, John O. Potter resided in Foster.

come I shall write to you or M tell Ida that the thing I send home I will send to Edwin for the Baby I should like to see him I like the name Waty reposes as well or the best of the list as for Wm it would be old Bill or young Bill it would be Bill at any rate now with much love to you all I will close yours truly and affectionatly Wm. O Harrington

Letter IX. *Harrington recalled in great detail the part performed by the Seventh at the Battle of Fredericksburg*

Fredricksburge V.A. Dec 16th 1862

Dear Wife
    we are back in our old camp again this morning and having health and leasure I thought I would write you a few lines to let you no that I am all safe and well although may have fallen it will be useless to attempt A description of the seens of the few past dayes I will only sat that it was awful Wednesday we ware ordered to be ready to start at eny time on three dayes rations thursdey our arilery opened fire on the city at 5 am and up a heavy fire all day just at night some of our troops crossed over into the city Friday morning we ware ordered to cross overe and at 9 ½ am ware in the city the rebbils had there artilery placed so as to rake the streets running back to the river making difacult for us to move with safety we had quite a number of men wounded while crosing the streets at night we slept in the streets saturaday morning we ware formed in line and at noon marched onto the field through a murdereous fire of shot and shell but we did not flinch we held the front of the line for 6 hours I was in the front with George Potter he was wounded in the shoulder slightly John Austin is wounded in the neck bad but will probily get well I have not seen John since he was taken from the field he was taken back acrost the river and I here has been sent to Washinton about one third of out regt is

dead or wounded we had all our field officers killed or wounded excep Col Bliss lieut Col Sayles[58] never reached the field he was killed with a shell it time to write about something els if I live to get home I will tell you more about the Battle I think I shall remember it some time we got back to our old camp last night I rather feel old something as if we had A hard days work old and stiff keep selling off if you can get the price and get all the money in gold and silver if you think best to sell the old colt sell her and the wagon if you think best I cant advise you for I dont know what is going on in your line of buisness do as you think best amounghest you I will send this little book to pappys man and the others to fathers lady I picked them up in the street my love to all your one husband William

Letter X.

Fredricksbergh Dec 17th 1862

Dear Brother

    I take this oppertunity it being the first offered you will see at once that I am alive and am well through the blesing of the God of battle I was spaired though our short stay on the other side of the river I cannot discribe the seenes that we have passed through we crossed over the river friday morning the city was shelled thursdey al day the cannon kept up a constant roar all day long but Friday they would only fire on our troop when they ware crosing the river the rebels had there guns placed so as to rake the Bridge and all the streets running back from the river makin it dangerous for our troops to move while we had no chance to hurt them we had to sleep in the streets friday night saturaday morning we ware formed in line we had several killed and wounded

---

[58] Lieutenant Colonel Welcome B. Sayles of Providence was hit in the chest by a shell fired from the Washington Artillery as the Seventh entered the field.

before we left the city at 12 clock we mooved forward to the front off the line ½ mile back off the city under a heavy fire all the way we lost of our regt killes and wounded before we got to the front from 1 o'c till dark when we were called off the field it was a sad day I hope to never have to see another like it our boys did well Col Bliss sayed when we got back that night to the city Boys I make you a speech but say you have done your duty faith fully to day and have covered yourselfs with glory and honor we ocucped an old stone ware house for our quarters sat night and Sunday Monday noon we formed in again what was able not quite 2/3 as man as there was saturaday we went just at night towards the field I expected to see the same sight tuesday but was very hapily disappointed as we ware out only on picket we ware called off in the night and sent back acrost the river to our old quarters where I am now writing but moust close this for I must to Laroy to night so good by for the presant write soon and excuse the flawed sheet for I cant hardly think what I want to write I will tell you more if we wer meete for I shall never forget the scenes of the firs Battle yours truly Wm. O Harrington

Letter XI. *This letter was written to William's sister Melinda.*

Dec 18th 1862
Camp Near Fredricksburgh

Well Melinda

I think I will write you A few lines as I have a few spare moments this morning we have had A fight with the rebs and I think we have got the worsted as we have gained nothing but have lost quite a number of men killed wounded and missing near 200 from our regt they fel all round me but I was spaired without harm for which I hope I am truly thankful to the God of battle for his murcies and care we left our old camp friday morning and crosed the river into the city the city was left by the enimy so our troops had a good chance to get things the stores ware broken opene and the goods flung into the streets there was all sorts of stiff flung out into the mud if so I could have sent home a peanno[59] I could have got it easy enough but they wont let a feller send any thing home you will git the particulars of the battle before you will get this and I will say more about it that that it was blody I thought I would go over an se the Bois in the 21st this morning but cant git time as I am on extra duty to day I saw Wm Coal[60] the next morning after we got back to our old camp those things come those things come through safe the vest & night cap fit first rate I am warring the vest now I have hardly got used to the pockets yet but find them very handy all the things just come in play and I am greatly oblige for them I have not thought to mention them to Eunice she noes that I have got them I wrot home Tuesday but did not think of them things Solomon did not go to VT did he I want to here something about him if you go down to Foster carry this with you my love to all for I must close this as they are calling for the mil now I should like to fil the sheet but cant and must say good by for the presant write soon and please your old friend

    Wm O Harrington

Letter XII.

                Fredricksburge Dec 21st 1862

---

[59] As the city fell into Federal hands the men ransacked the city. The provost guard did little to prevent it.
[60] William Cole was the brother of Henry S. Cole whom was killed at Fredericksburg.

My Dear Wife

        it is with pleasure that I now seat myself to write a few lines to those I so dearly love on this fine Sabath morning I always feel nearer home when writing to you than at any other time my health continues good and hope these few lines find you all the same we have had quite A coole spell of weather but it is warmer to day those mittins & vest come in play even the nite cap in fact it all come in the rite time and I am very much oblige to you for it all I got another pair of gloves last tues they ware good buckskin and I gess come from Laroy as I got a letter from him the same mail not heard from Sanford since and have wrote to Josiah Laroy and Melinda since I wrote you last you see I can find some time to write in there is no one that should tell shor glad I should be to hold you all but cant tell when that time will ever come not very long if we dont have better sucess then we did one we ago Saturday I can see nothing in the battle accept a failer or a defeat John Austin has been sent to washinton did not see him after he was wounded Amongst the killed was Albert Winsor Ira Winsors son no one saw him fall and it was none was knone of him but they think that he is amongst the killed Georg Potter has not been on duty the past week oing to a slight wound in the shoulder he will go on duty sone I would have my picture taken and send it to you but it would cost me one dollar and they are giting scare out here at present I have between 4 and 5 $ and dont kno when they will pay us off I have hoped to git it by this time so as to let you had it to use when you wanted it but there is no signs of paying off I think that if they dont I shant spend it and will send home for thing that I want if you have sent my boots just mention it in you next letter keepe some of your sausage for me when we get some place where we can box through direct I will send the 4th certificate so that you can get the money the first of next month[61] I hope you can git this as to use it when you take up that mortgage if I was in your place I would sell what I could to a good advantage off the stock that I did not want but do as you think best I have not got a letter from Elisha yet there I gess that I will close take good care of yourself and children Dear things I should like to see and kiss them but take good care off them and if is gods will we shall all meet again my whole love to you all & best respects to Neighbors & friends

from your one husband Wm O Harrington
our Capts name is George M Durfee

Letter XII.

Fredrickburge V A Dec 28th 1862

Dear Brother
having a few spare moments this morning I thought I would write you a few lines to let you kno how I am gitting along my health is good as usual and have a good appatite & but little to eate since we got back from fredrick we have not had more then half rations our bil of fairis coffee for breakfast A small piece of pork for dinner once and while rice for supper not very oftine this has been our fair most of the time since we recrossed the river our daily rations of hard bread are from 7 to 11 per day we hope to get a better fair soon it is quite warme and pleasant and our Boyes have got quite lively again our wounded have most all been sent to washington so there is nothing to remind us of our sad excursion but our thind ranks and the loss of familiar faces we are all lying perfectly still except picket and gard duty which takes 2 coyes out of 10 for our regt to picket the river

---

[61] In order to collect their monthly town bounty the men had to prove they were still in the service.

bank there is no signes of our going into winter quarters yet as I can see but what the next moove will be I cant tell but am in hopes that we shall not have to fight another battle this winter if we do the 7 will do her part if well officered the most of our officers ware half drunk and some more than that when we marched onto the field but most off them got sober before they left I dont think that they can get but few of them on a field if sober I have been thinking that they would pay us off but see signs of there doing yet I have got prety near out of spending money if you have got 3 or 5 treasurey note to spare you may send it to me and charge it to me I here the paper money in R I is twenty-five cents on the dollar if so Mother will go crazy I gess I got a letter from Learoy last night that they are all well but say that they have not heard from yo in some time I shall write to him to day I gess I have sent home after a pair of boots to come in George Potters box as soon as we get into quarters some where I shall try to get a box with something to eat in it our col name is Z R Bliss Capt Geo M Durfee 1st Brigade Gen Nagles 2 Div Gen Stugess 9th Army Corps Gen Wilcox there is some signes of another fight as there is firing up the river it may not be any thing searious I hope it wont but if we fight I will try to write you soon after the battle I must close so good By

Yours truly and affectionatly
Wm O Harrington

Letter XIII. *With the Battle of Fredericksburg over, the Seventh settled down to their miserable winter at Falmouth.*

Fredrickberge Jan 2nd 1863

My Dear Wife
it is with pleasure that I now take my pen in hand to write you A few lines to let you no that my health continues good and that we are getting along very well it looks now as

if we should winter here although most of us would prefur to get nearer to Washington for winter quarters then we should be in A more direct line of communication with home & it would release us from A good deal of picket and other gard duty but we have learnt to take thinks as they come and shall be contented to stay here we have had very pleasant weather most of the time once and while we have A cold snap but not as cold as is in R I we have not had mutch stormy weather so far this winter the wounded have all been sent off to Washinton so we have nothing but our thinned ranks & loss of familar faces to remind us of our loss or to fainting I did not think of it if I had hardly think I should have dast to as I was not hit and had but little time to watch the killed and wounded which ware very plenty all around me several times the blood from others came on me but I am very thankful to think that I escaped unhurt you spoke of sending some meal in that box if you git this before you send it dont sed the meal but you may send me A salt we can get meal and flower boath out here some butter would go first rate and a two quart tin pail would hold 3 or 4 lbs and some fried cakes if A little dry would be quite A rarity but dont wory if you sent the box I shall be very thankful for what it contains I don't what it is I have sent the children something & will send you something for a New years presant and shall send one to Waty when we git paid of so that I can have some money to spair we have been living rather short for some time bit are living better now give my love to your self and children Wm.

Letter XIV.

Fredrickberge V A Jan 11th 1863

My Dear Wife

it is with pleasure that I now take my pen in hand to write you a few lines to let you no that I am stil enjoying the best kind of health & that every thing remains quiet on the Rappahannock your letter of the 1st come to hand last night & it was with A very thankful hart that I read the good newes that you are al well and seme to be injoying your self so well and only wish that I was at home with you to ad to your happiness I feel very sory for Henry Call[62] I dont no what should I do if I was in his place or if sutch news should be brought to me I pray to God that no sutch newes will ever have to be brought to me and that in his one good time he will allow is all the happiness of the meeting again I hope that you wount deprive your self of any thing that will add to your comfort and the happiness of the children but be careful of your self them and dont go where you will expose the children to any disease unnesaryly we have got oure house fixed up for comfort with a fire place in it now it looks live A coal cabin and is very comfort able we have but little duty to do and so the weather has been very good most of the time yesterday it rained all day so we had A chance to stay in our houses all day 4 of us occupy one tent or house we have been living rather poorer then common for some time but are doing better now the railroad had been verry buisy gitting off the wounded and hospitall stores so they could not bring us our provision one off our boys had A box come to him with ham, sausage, butter, cheese, fried cakes & dried apples and George & I have bought some of his groceries and lived first rate we had to promise to sell off some of our stuff when it come if the box had not been sent when you get this may putin some thing for allspice cloves sinamon or some sutch things for some thing if you have sent the box send a little at a time when you write fold it up in you letter carefully insted of stamps as I have plenty of stamps at presant if you should

---

[62] Henry S. Cole's remains were never recovered.

get this before you send the box you may put in some sausage cheese butter fried cakes and any thing that is good to eate and that you think will keepe and I will settle with you when I come home I found one dollar in that letter last night dont send any more for there is no money that will readily here but tresury nots and I dont nead but little mony out here if I git the box with something to eate I dont no as I shall ness any $ now good night with mutch love to yourself and children I remain your true and loving husband Wm O Harrington

Letter XV. *While the Seventh was suffering at Falmouth, the citizens of Rhode Island made plans to send a schooner loaded with fresh provisions to the regiment.*

Fredricksburge V A Jan 21st 1863

Dear wife

After waiting longer than usual for A letter from home I have got one from Mother wrote and Mailed at the phenix[63] and was very glad to here that you ware all well at home and down there to she sayed that Leroy had send a box to me in the schooner that was to bring out vegatibels to the R I troops and we here that she had got in to the harber at Bell plains 6 miles from here if that is so we get the boxes soon if nothing happens Mother sayes the baby is the handsomest and most active of eather of the children at his age I cant help thinking that you must have your hands full with all three the lord bless them how I should to see them and all the rest of you now about the place mother write that Uncle Rhubin want the place and Albin want it to now if I Albin has it you will have all the house to your self and not have Aunt Abby nor Oscar to get along with ther if Albin

---

[63] Phenix was a village in Coventry, Rhode Island.

will feed the hay and fat the pork on it I want as mutch of the grain fed on the place as well as the hay if you think best to let uncle R have it if Albert let him have it anny body els that wants it onley lookout for your self as to Albert you must use youre one judgement if I was at home I should like to keepe him if he minds well and works well you might keep him to tend your garding and plant a little or els bet Melvin find him A place I cant give you any advice for dont no half as mutch about farming in R I as you do and had rather trust to your judgement than my one my whole time is taken up so that I dont think I will do for me to interfere withe the place do the best you can and get Elisha to helpe you by the way I have not heard from him I should like to kno whether Mr Ira Winsor gits his sones bounty since the battle of Fredericksberge not give him my address and tell him to write me we are haveing a regular old northe easter to day it began to rain last night at darke & rained all night and so far to day it is 3 o clock and as usual out here the mod & clay is to or three inches deep and makes me think of A sposhy snow at home when about half frozen rather disagreeable there now I will close my health continues the first rate give my respects to all with mutch to your self Mother & the children ah how well I should like to see you and kiss your self and children now good night my Dear
From your William

Letter XVI. *Burnside proposed to march his army up the Rappahannock in an attempt to outflank Lee's Army. Instead the rain fell for nearly a week, bogging down the army in the mud. The morale became so broken, that hundreds of Union soldiers deserted. It was one of the darkest times for the Army of the Potomac.*

Fredricksberge V.A. Jan 25/63

Dear Wife

your very welcome letter of the 18th got to camp yesterday & one from Melinda but I did not get them untill to day noon for we was out on picket yesterday & got back to day my health is good yet and am very glad to hear that you are all injoying the same great Blessing we have been expecting another Battle here or some where in this neighborhood and should have had if it had not stormed for one devision had mooved and we had our three dayes rations delt out and orderd to be ready at minuts notice to march but it began to rain the 19th at night and rained until noon the 23 part of the time the storm was quite seveir it has made it so muddy that they could not moove there artilery & pontoon briges round in season so the enemy learn our plans got along reinforcement ready for us and our troops have returned to there quarters again I hardly think we shall attempt to move again for some time the troops that mooved were out through the while storm got back yesterday they say they had a very hard time of it and I gess they did it was so mudy that the waggons would settle to the ground in the mud & the cannon had to have 10 horses to each one and then they could hardly moove them some they had to ty long ropes to and then the men would draw them out I will tell you more about it some time I am expecting my box every day when you send yours put in some chesse, butter, sausage, dried apple something for spice & 3 or 4 lbs of sugar when we get sugar we git a spoon ful for one day I think I wil write agane before you send it our fare is rather poore and had been for the last month [Some fried caks would go first rate] I think I will send you one of our hard beads we have 10 for one dayes rations and a small piece off pork one spoonful of sugar & one of cofee is our marching rations when in camp sometimes we have a few beenes and some times rice the whole army are gitting along disadisfied with there fare & pay for they hant had no money for some time & no signs of gitting along Melinda sent me her picture it look very mutch like her if I had your and the childrens taken that way they would be A treasure to me but it would be impossable for me to keepe A Deguaretype they are oftine sent to the troops but soone git broken it was hard worke for me to burn up the letters that I have had from home but did it one week ago today I never hated to doo anything worse but did not want the rebs to git them as they might if we had crossed the river I saw the 2 VT regt yesterday the 2 and 5th [64] whitch reminded me of Arey[65] what regt and company is he in if I should fall in withe his regt I should like to get acquainted with him so now good by withe love to you self and the children I remain your loving husband Wm O Harrington

Letter XVII.

Fredrickberge Feb 1st 1863

My Dear Wife
    I will taker A few moment this after noon to write you A few lines my health is very good in fact I believe that hard fair & soldiering agree with me for I am groing my cloaths my dress coat I cant hardly button now when I first come out was qute loose it cant be good living for that we dont no I ment to send you one of our cakes or hard breads they are pies and all sorts of flower victuals in one uncle john can offorde A soldier now I got your letter of the 25 last night and was very glad to hear that you was all well and giting along well I gess you wel get to be so mutch of A busines waman that you wont want anyone to oversee your farm for you when the war is over but you may get hard tell

---

[64] The 2nd and 5th Vermont was both part of the Army of the Potomac's Sixth Corps.
[65] Unidentified

Ida I want her to piece up A prety quilt for me and soo it good for I still think I shall be at home after it with in one year from the time I left I expect Josiah is at home before now I hope he will stay until he gets thouroughly restid the rainy season has sat in I believe for it rains half of the time and clowdy all the time I have ben watching for good weather to have my picture taken for Melinda & Waty they have paid off some of the regt in our Brigade one month pay 13 $ when they owed them 10 $ or more I never work where the pay was so poor before but I believe I borrow as little trouble as any one but the whole army is dissadisfied I think this letter is the tru sentiment off the whole army the schooner onboard which Leary put my box had gone to the bay I guess I have got tiard of wating for it and you may send one by expres as soon as you please take your on time and remember that I can git along with out any of the things I should like some butter chese dried apple sausage some sugar ¼ pound yea the butter and cheese will keep and they have commeneced to build some ovens today & that looks as if we ware going to have some fresh bread for us to butter A few fried cakes and fill it up with what els you please In the eating line that will keep it takes 7 or 8 dayes for A box to git here it wants the same directions as a letter only had 1st Brigade 2nd Division 9 Army Corps with much love to you all I remain your loving husband William

Letter XVIII. *The Seventh was transferred to Newport News in a plan to open up another front against Richmond, in addition to relieving them of the suffering at Falmouth. The letters addressed from Harrington to "Dear Brother" are to Josiah Harrington.*

Newport News Feb 13 1863

Dear Brother

I got A letter from you last Sunday but have been so buisy eversince that I have not had time to write before we arrived here the 11th after being two dayes on the way this is A very pleasant place all though we miss our old quarters but still think the Boys are better sadisfied here than they ware at Fredricksburg and A good deal better fellings prevails amoungst the men you causioned me to be on gard against talking to mutch I write more than I talk for I have seen enough to learn me that there was nothing maid by falt finding except the displeasure of your officers whitch I have mot got yet I have never had one of them speake A cuss word to me yet in fact I think I am giting along finely take it all around I got a letter from home this morning Eunice wrote that you thought of coming back to your regt about the 1st of Feb I am sorry that you could not stay at home longer so as to get rested and get your health recupted better this place reminds me of camp Bliss R I the riging of the Cumberland[66] is still in sight out in the river where she was sunk by the Merrimack we are fairing better now than we have sicne the battle at F we have soft bread fresh beef & salt beef white rice & beanes against hard bread and salt pork at our old home near Fredrickb I must write to Sanford & Laroy & one home tomorow so must close this yours truly and sincerly William O Harrington

Letter XVIII.

Newport News Feb 26th 1863

My Dear Wife having A few spare moments this afternoon I think I will commence A letter I am in good health and sprits for last night I got my box that you sent the thing ware all in good shape except the mince pies they ware already moldy

---

[66] The U.S.S. Cumberland was sunk by the C.S.S. Virginia at the Battle of Hampton Roads.

so that there was nothing good but some of the middle of them I carraid Capt Kenyens cake to him he is now Capt of Co A[67] he is a fine fellow I stayed and talked so long that I could not write until after brigade drill yesterday we had A review of the whole 9 army corps it was splendid sight to se 20,000 troops all mooveing in one body George got his box last night to his pies ware spoilt Edward Lewis[68] another tent mate of ours got one to his pies ware all spoilt to they ware all packed to gather like mine if there had ben two thicknesses of paper between each pie I think they would have kept good but it did first rate as it was considering time it was carring I am afraid I shall out grtow all my cloaths before it is all up if I dont get sick by eating to much but will try not to for I never had better health then now I had as lives Uncle Rube would have the place as any one but Aunt Aby & Oscar may be troublesome if they are in the house [but I dont no] Jo wrote that the stock looke first rate how does Mother get along with the mortgage has she got it all straight I will try to behave well so as I come home to work for you when I get through with Uncle Sam now dont talk so sober about being cross or I shall think I have been finding fauly which I have not intended to they are giving leafs of absence to those that can give good reason for asking for it for 20 dayes I have no excuse except the loved ones at home and the parting would pay all though if I could get a furlow I should be tempted to come home but hope to get home some time for good give my respects to all take good care of your self and the children with much move I remain your true husband William

---

[67] Harrington refers to Captain David Kenyon; of Company I. Captain Edward T. Allen led Company A.
[68] Edward S. Lewis resided in Scituate. He was wounded at Spotsylvania and mustered out with the regiment.

Letter XIX. *With Burnside taking command of the Department of Ohio, the Seventh was transferred with him to Kentucky.*

Lexington KY Apr 2nd 1863

Dear Brother
   as I have a few spare moments this afternoon I gess I will write you A few lines we left Newport News last thursday morning at 1 oclock after geting payed of the night before it took us till we started to git on board the transports to Baltimore the next night at 11 oclock but didnot leave the transport until the next afternoon & then took the cars for Cicinati got there monday night got some supper then crossed the river into Covington & yesterday we landed here it has been rather a tiresome journey but we have seene quite a lot of the country I dont think we shall stay here long this is the best looking farming land I ever have seene things look some 3 or 4 week earlier than in R I the meadowes are quite greene I meant to write you when in B but was in gard that day & could not find time my health is good we got pay for 5 months 14 days 72.35 I sent home 50 $ and have 18 $ elft now and will send you some the next time I write I must close so good by yours truly Wm. O Harrington

Letter XX.

Camp near Richmond KY Apr 19th 1863

My Dear Wife
   After finishing my letter to you today I think I will give you a lesson from my daily journal Afternoon 60 of our regt ar ordered out on picket it is raining in showers Apr 20 had an uncomfortable night no shelter but it is clare and warm to day got back to camp at 5 oclock just in time for

dress parade we are excuse duty for half a day after being on gard 24 hours battalion drill this after noon battalion is one where the whole regt goes out and drills together it is clear and warm 22nd it is warm to day in drill this noon we are to get ready fort a general inspection this afternoon in the first place we are formed up in companies then march out and form the in companies then march out and form the regt our guns & acuipments are examined then our knapsacks are looked over then our tents if our guns & cleaths are clan and tents look to suit them it is all rite if not they have to be put in order right off they have never found any fault with our mess yet 23rd we had a stormy night last night Co drill this fore noon no drill after noon it is rany 24th Co drill this fore noon worked for Lieut Wilber[69] this after noon I should have to drill it is a battalion drill 25th there is no drill to day Saturdays are for cleaning up and getting ready for inspection Sunday our Chaplain[70] is about as good as a wooden man for we seldom see him acept tomorow we shall have an inspection and that is all the weather is warm as summer at home now out here we hant got so that we get our mail regular yet but I think that I have got every letter that has been sent except those that Elisha sent is he ever sent enny if one at home could se the rushing for letter when the mail comes to the regt they would never attempt to soldiers friends from writing by all meanes cant writeas oftine as covenent for I feel nearer home the oftine I heare from you about two weeks to get a letter from you the war newes is good there I have filled this shett and must stop I cant think that it will improve the neighbor hood by having Nates folks in it but Nate will be a god hand for you to hire to help you I had heard of Uncle Warners death by Geo Potters folks I

---

[69] Captain George A. Wilbur replaced Captain Durfee in the command of Company K.
[70] The chaplain of the Seventh was Harris Howard; he resigned on July 3, 1863.

have no feelings of sorrow to express Although I always liked him well but think he is out of his misery now if I had such a wife I should want to die take good care of your self and dont work to hard it must be hard work for you all to doo the choars and your one worke birds but I hope it wont always be so for I hope still to get home by fall good by withe much love to you all Wm O Harrington

Letter XXI. *As the Ninth Corps performed garrison duty in Kentucky the men began discussing where they might go.*

May 24th 1863
Camp near Crab Orchard Ky

My Dear Wife

  having a little spare time this morning I think I will write A letter or to and will begin by writing to the loved ones at home first night before orders come to be ready to start for this place at 6 oclock sat morning so we had an early breakfast consistin of hard bread salt pork & coffee shortly after six we formed in line and started it was warm and when we got here we looked laughable I can tell you it was impossible to tell whether we ware black or white as the dust and sweet sticking to our faces have got to be pretty thick you can bett that we raised quite a dust as the rods were very dry and there was some 5,000 of us besides three batterys and our times at crab orchard used to be quite a sporting place in times of peace here is a race course fair ground & A place for fighting roosters and doogs the last place is a sircle formed by a tier of seats built like stairs covered like sheads the village all on one streete and looks like some old factory village & it is prety secesh I gess we have splendid news Vicksburge this morning our force have taken 57 pieces we are to doo provost duty while we stay here long that will be we cant tell my health is first rate & Lieut Wilber sayes when they tire me and they wonts have many left Geo Potter is out on picket and has my ink so I have to write with a pencil our mail did not come up with us last night I am going to write to Melinda and have got to go out on patrol duty from 4 till 7 and must soon close I should like to come home and see you all the best kind but must see the war closed first or searve my time out some of our boyes went home on a furlow last week to stay 15 dayes it will cost them 50 $ to go and come back I think if they had sent there folks there money there folks would have been more contented themselves and stop take good care of yourself and the children with much love to you all I am Yours William

Letter XXII. *In need of reinforcements to bolster his army besieging Vicksburg, Mississippi, Ulysses S. Grant called for the Ninth Corps to reinforce his lines. The Siege of Vicksburg had begun in May and each day the Union forces starved the city into submission with a constant bombardment.*

Crab Orchard Ky June 3d 1863

My Dear Wife

as I have A little spare time to day and not knowing when I shall have another chance to I think I will write you a short letter I have been looking for A letter for two or 3 dayes the last one that I got was May 17th and was glad to heare you was all well my health is good as common I think that we are all about to commence A summer campaine and a sturing one to I dont know where we shall go to but think somewhere into Tenn yesterday we ware ordered to have all our extra clothing packed ready for the teams to take off to headquarters to stowaway all that we carry is one change of undercloths one extra pair of shoes sixty rounds of cartridges & eight dayes rations so you guess what we call light marching order what would one think in R I to start on an eight dayes journey and have to carry enough to last them to eat all the time I think that they would get tired the first tripp but we out here have got used to it and take it as cooly as one can where the thermometer stands between 75 & 105 and a chance for a little fight any day we may not leave here in a week and may go before nite when we do start we shall be so buisy that I may not have another chance to write for some time so if you dont here from me dont get uneasy about me we have learnt never to borrow trouble I dont no there is any newes to write that would be newes to you as you get it as soon as we do we are watching & waiting hoping soon to here of the fall of Vicksburge if Grant takes them there I think we shall have to clean them out off Tennassee I am not very sory that you did not get the childrens pictures taken although no one can tell how glad I should be to see them I oftine wake in the nite and lay and think of you all and wonder how the children have changed I am still in hopes of getting home some time this fall but I dont no them Rebbels seeme determined to bother us as long as they can let them do there worst it is only A question of time they must be subdued in time I am glad that this war is not in Northern states the people there know nothing of the sufferings of the southern states whilst the folks at home have all the luxuareys they have been used to in times of peace in the south they can live everything is very dere and rear we see reffugeese from Tenn every one and A day or two which have to run away to keepe out off the hands of the rebs they say that they have travel nites and keepe still dayes until they get within our lines our troops are much better off than they are our families are amoungst friend and plenty theres amoungst there enemies with but little to eate and they say it of no us to plant the do the rebs will get there crops unless we get out off the state there here comes George with a letter for me I must read it this is yours of the 23rd I am glad to hear it youre are all well and that you get along well it make time pass A great deal pleasanter know that you are doing well at home tell a to give the bill to the baby and she can have the ring tell he that I want her to be a little lady when I get home William

Letter XXIII. *Following their arrival on a steamer the Ninth Corps established their camps around Hayne's Bluff, Mississippi. Almost as soon as the regiment had arrived in the state the Rhode Islanders, unused to the climate began to fall ill.*

In camp Near Haines Bluff Miss June 17th 1863

My Dear Wife & family
    after a delay of two week I do again find time to write you a short letter we have been very buisy for the two past weeks riding about but here we are safe as yet and enjoyoing good health as usual I am getting impatient to hear form you as I have not had a letter since we left Kentucky we left our old camp at Crab Orchard at four oclock of the morning of June the 4th and marched to camp Dick Robinson 23 miles the 5 we went to Nickelos ville 15 miles the 6 we took in the after noon the car for Covington 110 miles just before we took the cars an engine burst killing 4 men and wounding 10 more badly one of the killed was of our Regt.[71] 7th we got to Covington this morn at 4 oclock and cross the Ohio river to Cincinnatti there took the car for Cairo 400 miles from Cin to Cairo we passed through the states of Ohio Indianna & Ill it Cairo we take the steamer dave off

---

[71] William Bently of Company A was killed in the boiler explosion in Kentucky as the regiment was preparing to embark for Mississippi.

Louisville Memphis 250 miles we stayed here one day and two nite waiting for oreders we got orders to go to Vicksburge 350 miles further down the Miss river so on the morning of the 12 we left Memphis at 4 oclock and landed at youngs point 6 miles above vicksberge at half past eight on the morning of the 14th nothing of importance on our voiage except occasionally we exchanged shots with the guirrellers we are where we can here and see the firing we ware orderd to warrinton tomorow to cross the river to help Grant but when we had got about half of our men over the river [for we landed on the side oparsite of Vicksburge] we ware ordered back for Genl Grant had enough there so at night we went back to our old camp and stayed all nite the morning we took the steamer St Louis for haines bluff 23 miles up the yazoo river we stayed onboard the boat all nite and this morning we landed and come out here two miles back from the river and piched our camp this is the place where Grant gained the first great victory the place was well fortified by the rebels there big guns still lay in the three breast works we went over to see them this morning two of them are very large some of our boyes have just come in from a stroole about camp and brought in lots of ripe black berreys and will plumes the corn is up to my chin the most new things to us out here is the live oak cotton wood & cane breake we are some ten miles from vicksberge tell Mr Sweete that I think I have seene some biger mudsprouts[72] than he ever did we have fished in the miss every chance we could get some of the boyes got some that weight eight lbs & half & look like little sharks give my respects to him if I ever get home and dont forget it I shal have to tell him A fish story or two I dont know of what will happen whill we stay here if the rebs attempt to reinforce vicksberge we shall have a chance to fight them if not we may get back to Ky with out fighting for I think we shall

---

[72] A type of catfish.

called back there as soon as vicksberge falls there I must close take good care of yourself and the children my respects to all and love to the very Dear ones at home I should love dearly to see you all and home to some time William O Harrington

Letter XXIV. *After spending several days digging trenches around Vicksburg the Seventh was ordered to their old camp. Vicksburg fell on July 4, and the Mississippi River was finally open to free navigation, and the Confederacy was split in two.*

Camp in the wood on the road between the Yazoo & Big Black rivers July 2nd 1863

My Dear Wife
  As Capt Jenks[73] of Foster is About leave for home I thought it would be A good time to send A letter home and not knowing whether them that I have sent by mail have got home or not I think I will write I have not had a letter since we left Ky & I am getting rather impatient to here from you my health is first rate I never felt better in my life we are in warm country but the weather seames to agree with me the first rate all of our company are quite healthy we are at work now cutting off the woods besides the rodde so as to letour cannons work over them we are to cut A strip 200 yards wide by the side of roade for 9 miles it is very hard the heavy timber yesterday was the first days work that was done on them they are to help keepe the rebs from Vicksburge it is

---

[73] Ethan A. Jenks was a native of Foster and commanded Company I of the 7th. He was dismissed in June 1863 on false accusations, but later returned in September. Jenks later saved the regiment from destruction at Spotsylvania and was brevetted major. He was wounded at Petersburg in 1864 and again in 1865. Jenks survived the war and became a lawyer in Johnston.

one of the most romantick places around here that I ever saw here is the fig tree the wild plum the pawpaw for fruite is for beauty there is nothing like the magnolia we are enjoying our selves the first rate the boys are all wishing to be at home to spend the 4th of July and telling what they would doo it is laughable to here them talk and calculate I think if I was at home I should be very apt to stay there we mis our male very much we cant get any papers to see so we dont know what is going on any where except here they keep firing on Vicksburge stedily but not very fast our folks keep gaining on them slowly Gen Grant could take them by storm any day but it cost a great deal more lives to doo it is so he will keepe off a good distance work with his big guns we are some 15 miles from the city but can here the firing very plane there is not the least doubt expressed as to our final success here it was rumored yesterday that we ware to report back in Ky in tenn dayes I dont know as there is any truthe in there I write enough I gess for once I gess I it will take you longer to read this than it do me too write it here is some Miss beenes and peese that I picked 3 or fore dayes ago I saw some greene corn yesterday take good care off yourselves my love to you all and A kiss for each one of you from William

Letter XXV. *After arriving back at Hayne's Bluff the Ninth Corps was dispatched to capture the Mississippi capital at Jackson. Here they fought a battle against Joseph Johnston's Army of Tennessee as they were marching to attempt to reinforce the Vicksburg garrison.*

Camp Jackson Miss July 14th 1863

My Dear Wife
    Again I have the opportunity to write you a few lines we are fighting Gen Johnson here or have been our Brigade have just been relieved after having been to the front 48

hours we have been very lucky we have lost only 2 men killed 10 or 12 wounded & some few taken prisoners[74] I have not been in the fight yet I am cooking for the Co and it has kept me very buisy our folks can shure off success all the time this morning the infantry ware ordered back out off the way of the artilery for our folks are going to opin on them with artilery to day everything is quiett but we are expecting to here them opin there fire every minute we have 60 cannon ready at any time it will make shot place for the rebs when they get to worke I am in the hopes that we shall not have to go to the front again I am as usual in good health and am in but little danger compared with the rest of the boys of our regt so keep up good courage as you oftine tell me I am writing on the only sheet of paper that George & I happen to have withe us as we left our writing materials all in our knapsacks 4 dayes since then we have had to ly on the ground with nothing over or under us but it is A warm place so we dont suffer much George is A sleepe while I am writing he has been to the front with the rest of the Boyes and has not slept any for two nites he is in good health and A good soldier to try to get word to Mrs. Potter that he is well and doing his duty faithfully these I have got to go to cooking fresh meet and gess I have wrote enough I have had to write on my nee on my old blouse doubled up the Boyes are all in good spritis and think that the rebelion is playing out fast good by my love to you all
yours truly Wm O Harrington

Letter XXVI.

Mill Dale Miss July 28th 1863

My Dear Wife

---

[74] Two of the wounded later died of their wounds. Company K lost one man wounded in the battle.

as we shall have a chance to send off letters tomorow I will write one or two my health is very good although there is quite a lot of sick one in the regt we are our old camp 2 miles from the yazoo river where we first went into camp in this state we went out 8 miles and worked on the fortifications until the 4th of July as soon as Vicksburge surrendered we started for old Jo Johnson then on the big Black river 22 miles off when we got to the river he had gone to Jackson 35 miles further on still we pressed him slowly so as to let other troops get a head of him so as to make him fight at Jackson for it was hard work to follow him the weather was so hot to march in we over took him and he showed fight a little then run his army is wholy demorilized hundreds of his men have left him and com into our lines they say there is a lot more that will leave as sone as they get chance and that they wont fight as they used to they are tired of the war we have had a hard time off it for the last three weeks the water has been very poor & scarce some time we had enough to ear some time not some time we had shelters to lay under some times not but here we are waiting for the transports to take us back to Ky I wish you could see A Miss thundershow we have had three and such showers when it raines it does rain in earnest and such ratling thunder I never heard at the north your very welcom letter of the 28 got here last saterday I was very glad to hear that you was all well and geting Along so finely dont work your selves to deaths long as you can get along without it I got a letter from Josiah yesterday the first I have had from him in six weeks he sayes his health is better then it was his Regt had a very severe fight for its first one[75] his address is London Franklin Co Penn I expect to send this to providence by our Major he is

---

[75] The 18th Connecticut fought its first engagement at the Battle of Second Winchester on June 10, 1863. The 18th lost 570 men, mostly captured.

going home on leave of absence[76] we shall leave hear as soon as we can to get boats to carry us off and I shall be weel pleased to go for I have seene enough of Mississippi I am cooking for the Co still you may think that we dont live very well by the one that cooks for us but the we doo besure about all we have to cook is meat Beens & coffee we have had plenty of green corn peeches & some appels and figs the war is carried on here to suit us when we find an old reb we then leave him some time if he is troublesom they burn his house we have burnt jeff davis house & his brothers to there we are having another shower with much love to you all I am your absent William

Letter XXVII. *After the campaign in Mississippi, the Seventh returned to Kentucky in a much worn out state. Burnside was going to take his army to invade eastern Tennessee. Due to its reduced strength the Seventh was ordered to remain behind. The sick men were transferred to Camp Denison, near Cincinnati, Ohio. Here death was a constant occurrence from the disease encountered in Mississippi; nine men from Company K would die from the disease suffered in Mississippi.*

Camp Near Nicklass Vill K y Aug 19th 1863

My Dear wife haveing A little spare time to day I guess I will write you A few lines in the first place I am enjoying my usual good health and have but little to doo I am cooking for our officers now and have been for some time past the Capt is off sick so I only have one to wate[77] on and am not camp

---

[76] Major Thomas F. Tobey. His health was destroyed by the Mississippi Campaign and he resigned his commission several months later.

[77] The Seventh received very few of the promised conscripts, most were sent to the Second and Fifth Rhode Island; thus allowing the Seventh to be continually low in numbers.

half of the time I live quite easy now am getting fat again I weighed 153 this morning so you see that I have held my one and little more your specking of thunder showers at home I doo wish that you could see just one Miss shower the two worst ones we had was when we ware at the big black river going to and coming from Jackson when we ware going we had just spread our blankets and laid down to rest after A hot & hard march 6 miles in the hardist rain I ever saw such thunder & lightning to but enough of showers I have heard from Josiah but once since the Battle of W I have wrote him fore or five times and will try again to morrow I dont know as I should no the Baby I guess I should know the rest of you you must remember I have never seene the baby the children must have all grone I wish I could see them it is all most a year since I last saw any of you I oftine wonder if I shall have to stay another year I hope & think not Wills folks have had quite a call from three family I wish som of the would come out to see us we expect some of our me to start for R I in A few days to bring out the conscripts to us we are in hopes of spending the fall around it is sayed that our Corps is reported unfit for duty by Burnside that we should not go into active service this fall but shall then we may take the field again with in A week a soldier seldom knows to day what is in store for him tomorrow with much love to you all I remain your husband ever yours Wm O Harrington

Letter XXVIII.

Lexington K Y
Sept 18th 1863

My Dear Wife
Your letter of the 6th was received Wednesday nite and I was very glad to get it for I had began to get quite uneasy about you for it for I had began to get quite uneasy

about toy for I had not had A letter from you in over three weeks I had begun to think that some of you was sick so you may bet that I was pleased to get your letter and learn that you ware all well my health is fist rate we just got settled down so everything looks comfortable and I am in hopes we shall spend the winter here I went down town yesterday to get my picture taken to sent to Waty & Melinda but come A shower before I got a chance to have it taken so now I shall have to wate A spell I got A letter from Josiah A few dayes ago he was still at hagarstown[78] & well as usual I did think of the Baby on his birthday and of the rest of you to as was one year and one day since I had seene any of you I think I have stayed away well for one that used to stay at home as well as I did I dont think I shall have to stay another year I hope not I should like to see you all I dont believe that Ida would remember me I guess Arnold wil have on all winters job in the swamp I am very glad Sanford did not have to com into the army if he had he would have some worn our the army is no place for sick folks or any kind but the toughest kind especily in the ranks we have left some of our boyes in every state we have been in it makes me feele sad to think of the past & how many brave boys have left there bones in rebbeland but the future looks bright the army is in good spirits everything looks like A successful campaign this fall if so the rebelion must end and with the fall campaign I hope it will be so I can come home to you all by spring with much love to you all I am yours affectuinately William

Letter XXIX. *The Ninth Corps moved into eastern Tennessee, while William Rosecrans Army of the Cumberland was defeated by Braxton Bragg and the Confederates at the Battle of Chickamauga; one of the bloodiest battles of the war.*

---

[78] Hagerstown, Maryland.

Lexington Ky Sept 25th 1863

My Dearest Wife
    your letter of the 20 was received to day at noon it was mailed the 22nd consequently has been but three days coming I am very thankful to here that you are all well and getting along so well I should soon get homesick if you did not get along well at home but as it is I am very contented my health is as usual very good and duty lite you will learn as much of the late fights in Tenn[79] as I can write and before you can get this we are lucky in not being a portion of the old 9th Army Corps are on there way to reinforce Rosecrance if they have not all ready got there you will remember that we ware ordered there some three weeks ago Rosecrans sucess is not what I hoped it would be but he has done very well for he has had to fight all the best troops in the Confederacy and had held his one if our other armeys would improve this time to struck while so many of the rebs have been sent to help Bragg they might gain som easy victory time will tell I hope to hear of the army of the Potomack doing something to believe that Rosecrans will come out victorious give him a full chance I have been very lucky so far this weeke I have received letters from Melinda Esther M Josiah and two from you one yesterday & one to day I should like to have been at home to have your cousin but not more so than to have seene you all give my best respects to all our Vermont friends & relatives that visits you I wish I was there to help welcome them but such duty keeps many A man from the pleasures off home I was down town Monday and got A half doz pictures and shall send one to Waty Josiah Melinda and Aunt Pell you may have the other two to

---

[79] The Battle of Chickamauga was fought in Georgia near the Tennessee border.

give away there I guess I will close with much love to you all
I am yours ever Wm O Harrington

Harrington owned this farm in Foster

Letter XXX.

Lexington Ky Oct 11th 1863

My loving Wife
    it is with the greatist pleasure that I spend a few minutes this afternoon in writing to my loved ones at home I am in better humor too day then I was last Sunday when I wrote yours of the 27th got here weds and one of Oct 4th come the next day it is strange that they cant send the mail regular they are mean and careless but they are here now and I am very thankfull to here that your ware all well and getting along so nicely my health continues the first rate it does appear now as if we was in luck when we ware sent

here Lieut Colonel Arnold[80] told the boys last week that he thought we should stay here all winter and they had better fix up there quarters but still we may have to goany day I think that you did have prety near a house full of company I wish I could have been there too some time I allmost immagin my self at home farming if it want so far I ould come home nights and help you pic apples these long evenings but it is so far I wish I was General so I could afford it I would have you all come out and spend the winter in Kentucky with me the folks out here never guess at anything they always reckon if you meat one and ask him how far it is to any place he will tell you it is a right smart distance I reckon right smarts and I reckon seems to express a good deal with them if you ask them how mutch corn or potatoes they rase they will tell you keeps a bit I reckon it was quite amusing when we first come out here but we dont notice it now so much George has sent home to have his wife make him a pair of shirts and send him if she can get time to make me a pair and can find dark flannell you may send me a pair the army shirts are too short to suit me if you have a lot of socks on hand send out enough to last George and me all winter that is all the clothing I neede this winter my vest is god yet we can get shirts & socks enough but are awful poor if you send them see Mrs Potter and send all the things to gether in one box direct it the same as you do our letters send the pictures when you can for I want to see how you all look I am sory that you did not get the Babyes taken sio I could have seen his three I must close good night my darling Wm O Harrington

---

[80] Lieutenant Colonel Job Arnold was formerly a captain in the Fifth Rhode Island before being promoted to the Seventh. He contracted an illness in Kentucky and resigned in May of 1864; he died of the disease in 1869.

Letter XXXI. *Harrington was promoted to company cook in October. In this position he was relieved of guard duty and payed an additional forty cents per day.*

Nov 1st 1863 Lexington Ky

My Dear Wife
 your very welcome letter of the 25th containing yours and the childerns pictures was received last night I am very mutch oblige for them yours is not as good as Ida & Edwins but I could easyly tell whose it was I got those that you sent first got here last Tuesday so I had all off my family with me now in miniature Ida and edy look well and make the handomist picture that I have ever seene since I have been out Edwin looks the best I should have known Idas wher but Edys he is out goring my memory how all of the children gro and then they look good and healthy Shouldent I like to see you all George and I oftine talk of coming home some time we talke of coming in the spring if thing dont look more like peace than it does now but there is time for changes betwixt this and next May if it was not for coming back I would not wate till spring but that is where the trouble is it not that I should not love to come home but hate to leave you A gain I should love dearly to spend the winter at home with you but stern necessity compells me to fore go the pleasure tell Ida all that I can send her this time is a Farthers love but when I write again I will try to send her some thing we are expecting to be paid off again this weeke I am cooking for the Co there is 32 men to cook for now it keeps me quite buisy as there is no one to help me I will tell you how we live we have soft bread, coffee three times a day fresh beefe 3 or 4 dayes in et week sometimes boile sometimes bake it we dont have fresh meat we have salt beef or porke we have some cabage & potatoes then we have a boiled dinner rice George and I by two quarts of milk every night and have bread & milk for

supper milk is 5 cts a quart so you see we have supper there is no newes to write and will close except my whole love to your self and the family truly yours William

Letter XXXII. *The Seventh closed out 1863 still remaining encamped near Nicholasville, waiting for the events of the next year.*

Camp Nelson Ky Dec 28th 1863

My Dear Wife
  yours of the 20 was received to day and read as usual with much pleasure it is so pleasing to heare that you are all well and geting along so well my health is first rate with the exception of homesickness I have to one that I am troubled some with that just now we got here Saturday noon it began to rain Sat night and has rained ever since and it real mudy but here we are cooped up in our shelter tents [let me describe them they are made out of common sheeting it is twice the width of sheeting and a little more it cong longaway to make it square each man has one piece they are fixed so as to button togeather then we get two croches and a stick them down put a stick a crost then put the tent on that frame the ages of the tent are then pinned to the ground in this shape Δ that is our house I expect that we shall start again tomorow for we are only waiting teames to take the baggage it is reported that we are to go to Knoxvill the Regt is very much dissadisfied with the moove I dont think that half of the boys will be found whenb they are wanted I shall have to stop A kis apiece for you all W.O.H
Direct as before for a week or two untill we get some where

Letter XXXIII. *The Seventh remained in its camp constructing winter quarters and recovering its ranks in preparation for the spring campaign.*

Point Isabel Ky
Jan 24th 1864

My Dear Wife
    again I seat my self to write you a few lines we are still here and I am in good health we have just got our quarters fixt up and seteled down comfortably but I dont think we shall stay here very long the past week has been very pleasant weather I have been very buisy the boys have all been very buisy since we have been here so I am cooking alone yet but soon shal have a hand to help me if we stay here the water is very unhandy besides I have just had quite a boil on one of my knees that made me some lame between all of my mishaps I have not had time to write it is thought now that we shall soon be ordered back from here as the 9th Corps are to be recruited and placed under there old commander Gen Burnside to take a new field some where it is rumored that the whole corps are to go to N York to recruit of we do I shall hope to get home before we leave there but there is nothing sertain about our coming east again yet I have been looking fir a letter from you for some days they have had some talk of reinlisting our Regt for three years or for the war that re inlist the veterans Bounty of 702.00 and thirty days furlough I cant think this was can last untill our first turn of service is out so I think that those that re enlist will make there seven hundred & 2 dollars quite easy what do you think Colonel Bliss is in command of this post there is but part of two Regts here besides ours making in all 8 or 9 hundred men there I guess I have wrote enough and will close with much love to you all and as kisses as you please to your self and children I am as ever yours William O Harrington

Letter XXXIV.

Point Isabel Ky Feb 21st 1864

My Dear Wife
Again after another week of health and comparative happiness I find my self seated and writing home to my loved ones yours of the 7th was received last Tuesday and I am very glad to heare from you every week if the newes is a week or ten days old it is very pleasant to get it I should like to see Geo Johnson an Mr Griffin as well as any two newighbors I left I should like to step in and take a dish of bread and milk with you for we cant get it here I intended this morning to have gone out into the country to visite a large cave six miles from here but it snowed and I gave up so I cant see the cave to day it is quite a place I guess by what they say of it I dont think the children would know me and I should know of them I should know Edwin and Elmer but I think should know Ida any where when I look at there pictures Edwin makes me think of Owen Brayton I guess Elmer takes after me dont you I got a letter from Sanford to day the first one for a long time and shall write to him this after noon it is very pleasant this afternoon George is reading and raising cane so it is hard work to write but I shall fastine the door when the boys all get out there is no newes to write and I will stop take good care of your selfes and healths yours truly
Wm O Harrington

Letter XXXV. *On April 2, 1864 the Ninth Corps embarked upon the trains and proceeded to Annapolis, Maryland as reinforcements for the Army of the Potomac about ready to embark on the last great campaign of the Civil War. Late in April they marched south from Alexandria, Virginia and the Seventh began the campaign to end the war.*

Camp of 7th Regt near Bristoe Station Va Apr 29 1864

My Dear Wife
    As I have a few spare moments this morning and not knowing when I shall have another chance I will try and write you a few lines we left Annapolis the 27 and since then we have been on the moove all the time except the day we stoped at Alexandria yesterday we passed the old Bull Run Battle field and Manassaus Junction and encamped last at or near Bristoe Station we are in line now ready to start again I got yours of the 17th last night and was very glad to hear that you ware well my health is first rate never better we are looking for hot worke before many days likely this will be the last chance I shall have to mail a letter in some time but doo not get sad nor bee disappointed for I will improve the first leasure to write you again we are ordered to fall in and I must close with much love as ever William

Letter XXXVI. *The Army of the Potomac crossed the Rapidan River and fought the Battle of the Wilderness on May 5-7, 1864; the battle was a draw. Ulysses S. Grant now commanded the entire Federal army and moved his army south to the small town of Spotsylvania Court House. The Seventh was not engaged until May 12. The regiment remained at Spotsylvania for a week, fighting round the clock in the pouring rain. From this day forward nearly one Rhode Islander would be lost every day in the hellish combat of the Civil War.*

Camp in the field Near Spotselvania C House Va May 20th 1864

My Darling Wife,

Again I am blessed with the privalage of writing you a few lines to let you know that I am safe and well at presant we have had stirring times out here for the past 11 dayes most of the time we have been in the front lines of our army and are now at the front lines but we changed our position yesterday and are where the bullets dont fly so plenty as they did the day before yesterday we lost 6 killed and 18 or 20 wounded the only two wounded in our company was Nye [severly] & Lewis [slightly] boath good boys[81] we fight them some where on our lines every day how long this fight is going to the last the boys only knows bit I hope not much longer the men look weary and tired but are very cheerful we have got the best of them so far and have all confidence in an ultimate suceess I got two letters from you yesterday one March 20th the other May 1st am very glad to hear that you ware all well or nearly so Mr. Lewis lives at Chestnut Hill[82] it will be some time before or may be you get them things for I told Edward not to have him be to much trouble to forward them as there is nothing that would spoile I dont hardly know how I could set my self to work in a farm again if I was at home being used to so much company out here Mother does seame to hold out well to travel she would make a good hand march some times I get uneasy about your out doars worke and wish you had kept Albert with you or got some one els to done the chores but you have had your way Ida questions as to when I am coming home A hard one to answer tell Eddy to take good care of his stock untill I come it is late so I must close I have not heard form Jo in some time and dont get time to write only to you now with much love to you all I am as ever very truly your husband William O Harrington PS George is safe and well

---

[81] Company K's casualties at Spotsylvania were killed: Isaac Nye and George Simmons. Wounded: Abel B. Kenyon, Edward S. Lewis, Esais Pray, Jospeh Parker, and Chester P. Rounds.
[82] A village in Glocester, Rhode Island.

Letter XXXVII. *The Seventh continued to fight and fought engagements at Mechanicsville and Bethesda Church on June 1 and 3: one third of the regiment would go down in the brutal struggle.*

Camp in the Field Near Pamunky River June 2nd, 1864

My Darling Wife,
    As I have a few spare moments I will write you a few lines my health is good and hope this will find you all the same we have had stirring times ever since the 10th of May we have either been marching or fighting or fortifying most of the time night and day but the boys are very chereful every thing considering since I began this leter Corp Reynolds has been brought in dead shot through the head[83] so now both of my boys are gone killed the other wounded I dont know how many we have lost in all nearly 20 killed 60 or 70 wounded these are the times that tries men since we have been under the fire of rebiel guns but we are gaining on Richmon we are within 12 miles of it now and expect to moove again this afternoon I am cooking still have no gun and when our boys are fighting or fortifying I find some place where it is as safe as I can find to cook in when I am in the rear I have to carry things to them three times A day generaly go about daylight noon and night or at sutch times as there is the least fireing I see by what RI papers have seene you get the news and prety correct to tell Mrs. Potter if you see her that George is well I have got yours of the 8th and was glad to hear that youre health ware good and geting along so well and hope that we may be spaired through this rebelion to meat in time of Peace the troops are mooveing by

---

[83] Corporal Edward S. Reynolds of Scituate was killed in action at Mechanicsville on June 2, 1864.

and I must close with much love to you all and A kiss for each I am as ever truly yours Wm. O Harrington

Letter XXXVIII. *The Seventh continued to advance south and fought another round of horrific fighting near the Cold Harbor battlefield. Company K and the entire regiment continued to lose men at a terrible rate.*

June 4th 1864

Our mail did not leave as expected so I will mention a part of what has happened since I wrote we left on the 2nd at one oclock went about 2 miles and stoped to rest when the rebs pitched into us we ware having a heavy shower of rain at the time the fight was short but severe our regt did not get into the fight that day but yesterday at sunrise our regt advanced in line of battle and while crossing a swamp in the woods the rebs opened on but we crossed the swamp in good order and took up our position in front the fight has been very heavy Oliver Wood was killed in the morning shot dead he was the only one in Co K killed[84] we have 6 killed 40 wounded I was blest to receive your letter of the 22nd last night am very thankful for the god newes it brings write as oftine as convenient for it is very cheering to get a letter now I shall mail this the first chance I get W O H.

Letter XXXIX. *On June 15, 1864 the Army of the Potomac arrived at Petersburg, Virginia, only several miles from Richmond. Grant threw the entire Army of the Potomac against the heavily defended works of the Army of Northern Virginia. Robert E. Lee knew that he must hold this ground to save the Confederacy. After a week of horrific losses the Army of the Potomac began to besiege the town in a ninth month long operation. The Seventh Rhode Island was*

---

[84] Oliver Wood of Foster. James Taylor was mortally wounded, dying on July 15, 1864.

assigned to the far left of the Federal line; they were constantly under fire.

Camp in the Field Near Peters Burge Va June 22nd 1864

My Darling Wife
    Again I have a chance to write you a few lines your very welcome letter of the 12th was received yesterday and read with greate pleasure I cant find a bit of fault with you about writing for there is but a few that is a personal as you have been there is but little spare time with is now I am sorry that it is so that I cant write more regular but we have to take it as we can as you say there must be many mourning friends at home no one can realize it more than we can that every day we passed two our boys that had been killed in the night one cant tell what is to take place one hour ahead our boys are in the skirmish lines to day they are so clost to the rebs that when I carried our boys there coffee this morning the rebs hollowed and asked us if we had got hot coffee I told them we had and asked them to come up and take some with us but they thought we would shoot we can all most throw stones from our lines into theres our folks have got a deep ditch dug to walk up in and rifle pits when we get up to them I am cooking some wayes in the rear and are out of danger except when we are caring the boys there meales I should like to see you all the first rate it does seame funny to think that I have a boy all most two years old that I have not seene I oftine see the rest of you in my dreams night before last I was having a good time when the cannons made so much noise that they waked me up and I found that I was on the field in Va instead of being at home in RI I am glad that your money holds out for I don't know when I shall have any more to send there will soon be 4 months pay due us you did not perfectly right to take the deed in your own name I have land enough I hope Olney & Amanda will make a match

George is well and in the pits with the rest of the boys Capt Jenks was wounded slightly yesterday[85] I wish you could see one battle field then I should expect you to understand me when I write about them no one can understand it who has not seene it there is time for the boys to have there dinners and I will close with much love to you And a kiss for each I am as ever yours Wm O Harrington

Letter XL. *Throughout the month of July the men of the 48th Pennsylvania struggled to build a mine underneath the Petersburg defenses in an attempt to end the war early by blowing a hole in the Confederate works and storming the ramparts. Due to its reduced strength, the Seventh Rhode Island had been pulled off of the line and was assigned to the headquarters of the Ninth Corps. The mine was blown on July 30 and the battle became known as the Battle of the Crater. It resulted in a Union defeat. In the ensuing aftermath, both Ambrose Burnside and Zenas R. Bliss were relieved of their commands for their roles in the failure of the assault. Bliss was send to Wheeling, Virginia and was accused of not properly controlling his brigade. The Fourth Rhode Island Volunteers were heavily engaged and was nearly destroyed. At home in Foster, Harrington's wife continued to manage the farm, while William's brother Josiah resigned his commission and came home to Foster, deathly ill from his army experiences.*

Camp near Petersburge Va July 31st, 1864

My Dear Wife
    it is Sunday gain and will try and write you the news my health is as usual good and I am happy to learn by your letter of the 24th that you ware the same we fought the Rebels

---

[85] Captain Jenks was acting major of the Seventh.

yesterday and got whipt the fight began about sunrise by our folks blowing up one of the rebel foarts then they opened on them with artillery and musketry the fight was very severe we drove them out of two lines of there works when they broke and run and that broke the white troops and we ware drove back to our lines with a heavy loss they could not start us out of our own lines but if we had not trusted to the negroes we might have held our ground it is a sad sight to look over the field this morning it is fairly speckled with the killed and wounded that we cant get too take off the field they being under the rebel guns we lost none killed and but five wounded in our Regt it was not in the hotest part of the fight being on extra duty they had to carry each man one ax one spade and peck ax they ware expected to make fortifycations but had to give up there tooles and take there gunes to keepe the rebs form taking the works we had already made I am getting very uneasy about Josiah I have a part of the Chaplains letter that was in the transcrip Sanford sent it I should like some of your huckleberrys and milk first rate 44 $ seames quite a price for haying but help is very skerce and that makes wakes high did you have money enough to pay them it is very warm and dry out here my shirts are prety near worn out so you will have to send some this fall I am where I can get them take good care of your selves tell mother not to get to uneasy about Josiah he may not be soo bad as she fears I must stop now with love to all and a kiss to each Wm O Harrington
the fight ended about half past ten yesterday Am

Letter XLI. *Throughout the summer, Grant continued to squeeze Lee from his supply lines in a constant fight to cut the many railroad lines flowing into Petersburg and Richmond. The Seventh Rhode Island was engaged in the fighting around the Weldon Railroad.*

Camp Near Peatersburg Aug 22nd 1864

My Dear Wife

it rained so hard yesterday that I could not write ad I did not receive my customary letter but am looking for it every day I sent the other 15 dollars home by Maj Jenks as he was coming home to stay 30 days and sayed he would either send it to you or bring it himself so I am very sure you will get it we have mooved twice since I wrote before we are some five miles from our first camp we come here last Friday and tore up the Peatersburg and Weldon railroad and dont mene to let the Rebs fix it up again if we can help it they have tried twice to retake it but failed it rained most all last week the roads are getting mudy but a few fair days will dry it I saw John Johnson a day or two ago he is well he look like Elisha[86] he come over and stay an hour or too with me I have not heard any thing yet from Josiah or his Regt[87] I hope Major Jenks will call on you whilst he is at home every thing seames to bee mooving along finely in our army now the whole talk seames to be the armi stic all seam to hope that they will have one my health as usual is good and hope this may find you the same but I dont see why my letter is two days behind times I hope none of you are sick I should like to see and ask you how old I am today just to see if I am as old as I feele this wet weather makes me feele old then I should love dearly to see you all with love to all I will close yours William O Harrington

Letter XLII. *In late September 1864, Grant launched an all out assault against the Petersburg front. Lee beat the attacks*

---

[86] John Johnson resided in Moosup Valley with Harrington. He had saw service in the 11th Rhode Island and later joined Battery E, First Rhode Island Light Artillery.
[87] The 18th Connecticut was engaged in several important battles in the Shenandoah Valley and lost several men from Foster whom served in its ranks.

back with heavy losses, but bought several more months for the Confederacy. In addition Grant and the Army of the Potomac advanced closer to Richmond. The Seventh Rhode Island was engaged on September 30 at Poplar Spring and Hatcher's Run. This was also the last engagement of the Fourth Rhode Island.

Camp in the field Oct 3d 1864

My Dear Wife

Your letter of the 25 has been received and finds me in good health to and I am glad to hear that you ware all well and that Josiah was getting north again we have been having quite a moove out hear in fact we have been in motional the past week we come out here top look after the south side railroad and took one line of the rebels works 2 foarts 7 pieces of artiller and some priserners the 7th gained the honor of saveing the field the rest run but the 7th stood there ground we lost 1 killed and 3 wounded in our Co[88] they seam to be preparing for a big fight here soon if you get my things don send them as soon as you please the sooner that we shall leave this army soone put them in as small a box as convenient and direct it the same as the letters was you surprised to get a paper from me some time ago I sent it so as to let see the cotton plant I got a letter from Josiah yesterday he was in Ny but told me to direct his letters to Sterling so I expect he will soon be at home I am very buisy and have to write on the jump and mist stop now but will write soon again if nothing happens with much love to you all I am as ever truly yours Wm. O Harrington

---

[88] Company K's casualties were Stephen A. Clarke killed and only two wounded James W. Gavitt and another member of the company as yet to be identified.

Letter XLIII. *In November the Seventh Rhode Island moved from the left of the Federal line to the right at Fort Sedgewick, in addition to welcoming the one hundred and seventy veterans of the Fourth Rhode Island which greatly bolstered their ranks. On December 1, 1864 First Lieutenant Josiah V. Harrington finally succumbed to his illness and died in Foster.*

Fort Sedgwick Va Dec 15th 1864

My Darling Wife

Another week has passed and gone and I am still enjoying the great blessing of good health and was very glad to see by yours of the 11th which I received this morning that you ware the same and hope that we may continue so I feal very sad & lonesome when thinking of home but what is my loss in comparison to Charles Greenes I pity him from the botom of my hart there was a transcript sent to Geo Potter with the notice of Josiahs death in it it does me a Greate deal of good to hear him spoken of so well of and to think that he merited the good name that he fetched home with him I got a letter from Sanford Thursday he wrote nothing of Josiahs affairs how much we owe him I think we enjoyed the storm of the 10 & 11 tel Olney that I hope to see him keeping house when I get home Wm Wiley is in the hospital[89] some where that part of the 4th RI Regt that reinlisteed are with us but John Monroe is the only one I know in it that come from our parts[90] I think if ever live to get home that I shall try to get our grave yard fixed up or mooved if I had been at home and could had my way I would have bought a plot on the Plaines[91] I am glad Ida likes to go to school I should like to see you all very much I oftine wonder how the children looks

---

[89] William A. Wiley lived in Coventry and had previously served in the 4th Rhode Island. He was mustered out with the regiment
[90] John Monroe of Glocester served as a private in Company D.
[91] The Plainfield Pike ran through Foster.

and what they would think to see me I very oftine think of home a good feather bead & good old bead pellow but have no wish to have her share my bead of boards with me out here what want A man get used to now I can lay down on some boards and sleepe sound and easy as on a feather bead and if the bullets fly and canon roar a little it is all the same to us we have seene so much fighting for the past eight months that we care little for it now there was a salute of 100 gunds fired this morning in honor of Gen Thomases last victory in Tenn[92] there is but little newes here and I must close take good care of your selves and accept much love from your husband Wm. O Harrington

Letter XLIV. *After spending the winter of 1865 at Fort Hell, the Seventh prepared for the spring campaign. After the Ninth Corps repulsed a Confederate attack on Fort Steadman near Fort Hell on March 25, 1865 the die was cast for the final campaign of the Civil War. Early on the morning of April 2, 1865 the Seventh stormed out of Fort Hell into Fort Mahone, at the Confederate works and sent the Army of Northern Virginia out of Petersburg. This was the last engagement of the Seventh Rhode Island and they had performed with their usual ardor.*

Camp in the Rebs lines ¾ mile from Fort Sedgwick Va Apr 3d 1865

My Dear Wife
    I will just drop you a few lines to let you know that I am well we routed the rebs out of Petersburg yesterday the fighting began about 5 oclock in the morning and lasted all day but not very hard we are halted to form our brigade now in side of the rebs lines and shall start in Persute of the flying

---

[92] On November 30, 1864 the Union Army of Tennessee defeated the Confederate Army of Tennessee at Franklin and Nashville.

Rebels George is well we had none killed[93] in our Regt & but few wounded yours of the 26 has been received I was as usual very glad to here from you I never took a doller in the Army dishonestly excuse this letter and as soon as I get time I will try and doo better truly yours Wm O Harrington

Letter XLV. *After pursuing Lee to Farmville on April 7, the Seventh halted and waited while the Army of Northern Virginia surrendered on April 9 at Appomattox. Following the assassination of President Lincoln the Ninth Corps was dispatched to Washington D.C. in order to repel any rebel uprising.*

Camp Near High Bridge Va Apr 19th 1865

My Dear Wife

I will try to write to you a few lines to let you know that I am in good health and in hoped of getting home sometime I got two letters from you this week the latest the 9th I was very glad to hear from you and to hear that you ware well and as glad that Olneys wife was better and hope that nothing serious will happen to them if I am at home I will go after the Doctor when they get ready to pay up Only for running so when Ida was born we ware offisialy informed of the death of President Lincoln it has cast a sad shade on all our late victoreys there is not a man living that was more esteemed than was Father Abraham[94] but still was nothing but a good man and many a good man has lost his life since this rebelion broke out but I think the fighting is

---

[93] Four men of the regiment would die later of their wounds, amongst them were Major Peleg Peckham and Lieutenant Albert Bolles. On April 20, 1865 Private Richard Edwin Taylor of North Scituate became the last man to die in the Seventh Rhode Island.

[94] When the Seventh left Rhode Island in 1862 they sang the popular song, "We are Coming Father Abraham."

over now or so near over that we shant see any more of it in fact we have not seene any fighting since Apr 2nd from May the 12th to Apr 2d 1865 there was not two weeks put together that we want under fire but since then we have not sene an armed rebel we are waiting here for the rest of the troops to pass back they must have all passed and we shall soon be mooving back too there has been so much rain lately that the roads are all pretty bad so it will take us some time if we go back direct to Petersburge most every one thinks we shall be at home by July and I for one hope we shall if not before I dont know how soon I shall get a chance to send this likely tomorrow if not I will write more take good care of yourselves and accept much love from your husband. Wm O Harrington

Letter XLVI. *Following there participation in the Grand Review, the Seventh prepared to leave Washington and finally go home. The veterans were allowed to keep their Enfields, uniforms, and other equipments for the sum of six dollars. Private Harrington and indeed almost all of the men in the regiment sought to bring these treasures of the last three years of their lives home. The original three years men were mustered out on June 9, while the veterans of the Fourth Rhode Island came home on July 13, 1865. When the bloodstained and bullet riddled colors of the regiment were turned into the state authorities the Seventh Rhode Island Volunteers faded into history and memory.*

Camp near Alexandria Va May 21st 1865
My Dear Wife
    it is Sunday evening again and my weekely letter has not come it did not get my letter last weeke untill Wednesday now I shall scold somebody if they dont come regular but let it pass for I think this is my last letter home we are to go over to Washington tomorrow to be there for the review on the

23d and then we shall begin to think that we have got through soldiering our Colonel[95] have had orders to have the papers made out to discharge us immediately after the review so I think we shall be ready to start in about a weeke or so we have been having some pretty warm weather but it has been showery for two days and the weather is quite comfortable now I wish you could bee out here to see the review it is thought that there will bee 200,000 troops reviewed in boath days[96] it will bee a great sight my health is as usual first rate George is quite well if this finds you all in good health you had better not write again untill you hear from me again I am very much in hopes of being on my way home next sunday so will close take good care of your selves and accept much love truly yours Wm. O Harrington

William O. Harrington returned to Foster and continued to work on his farm. In his later years he became an active member of the James C. Nichols Post of the Grand Army of the Republic. Each spring these veterans would travel to the graves of their fallen comrades and place a small flag and group of flowers on the hollowed site. When William O. Harrington died in 1904, a motto of the Grand Army of the Republic served as his epitaph. It is indeed fitting for all of the men whom shouldered a musket and marched away with Company K, Seventh Rhode Island Volunteers. "For all that he was and all that he dared. Remember him this day.

---

[95] Lieutenant Colonel Percy Daniels.
[96] The Army of the Potomac marched on May 23, while the Army of Georgia marched on May 24.

CHAPTER EIGHT

Roster of Company K

The following roster of Company K is adapted from the one found in William P. Hopkins, *History of the Seventh Rhode Island Volunteers: 1862-1865*. This roster has been updated by this editor to include known dates of death of the members as well as information not included in Hopkins' original work. In addition, this editor has taken the liberty to insert the known burial locations of the members of Company K. After the war it was common for members of a company to move from the place where they had once lived. It is interesting to note that the men of Company K spent the rest of their lives living in the same communities in which they enlisted from. Today they remain buried in those communities.

Captain George N. Durfee. Clerk. Residence, Tiverton; enrolled Sept. 4, 1862; mustered in Sept. 6; resigned March 20, 1863. Died January 15, 1914. Buried at Tiverton Cemetery 65, Nannaquakeet Road at Pole 302, Tiverton, Rhode Island.

Captain George A. Wilbur. Promoted March 1, and mustered in as such May 1, 1863; detailed on special duty as a member of general court-martial at division headquarters Dec. 2, 1864; mustered out June 9, 1865. Died June 9, 1906. Buried at Union Cemetery, Smithfield Road, North Smithfield, Rhode Island.

First Lieutenant Gustavus D. Bates. Promoted from Co. E, May 23, 1863; discharged for disability Oct. 14, 1863; again commissioned first lieutenant Nov. 14, 1863; captain Co. E, July 25, 1864.

First Lieutenant Joseph Groves. Enrolled at Providence, and mustered in Sept. 4, 1862; transferred to Co. I, Jan. 13, 1863.

First Lieutenant Winthrop A. Moore. Promoted from Co. A, Jan. 9, 1864; acting adjutant from Jan. 13, 1865, until April, 1865; transferred to Co. D, Feb., 1, 1865. Died September 8, 1913. Buried at East Greenwich Cemetery, First Avenue, East Greenwich, Rhode Island.

Second Lieutenant Charles T. Healey. Commissioned Sept. 4, 1862; mustered in Sept.; resigned Jan. 7, 1863, and discharged. Died July 12, 1885.

Second Lieutenant John Sullivan. Promoted from Co. D, Jan. 7, 1863; acting adjutant from Jan. 22, until March 1; adjutant. Died 1904. Buried at St. Mary's Cemetery, Warner Street, Newport, Rhode Island.

Second Lieutenant Benjamin G. Perkins. Wheelwright. Residence. Wheelwright Promoted March 1, 1863; first lieutenant Co. A, July 1, 1863. Died July 28, 1898. Buried at Moschuck Cemetery, Central Falls, Rhode Island.

Second Lieutenant William W. Webb. Transferred from Co. B, Dec. 28, 1863; mustered out June 9, 1865. Died May 6, 1897. Buried at Grace Church Cemetery, Broad Street, Providence, Rhode Island.

Roster of Company K

First Sergeant George W. Bennett. Carpenter. Residence, Foster; enrolled Aug. 14, 1862; mustered in Sept. 6; wounded at Fredericksburg Dec. 13, 1862, sent to hospital and borne as absent sick until Feb., 1863; transferred to the Veteran Reserve Corps Oct. 31, 1863; mustered out with the non-commissioned staff of the 17th Regiment, Veteran Reserve Corps, June 30, 1865. Died May 6, 1881. Buried at Pine Grove Cemetery, Route 117, Coventry, Rhode Island.

Sergeant Stephen A. Harrington. Peddler. Residence, Scituate; enrolled Aug. 8, 1862; mustered in Sept. 6; absent sick from Oct. 27, 1862, until Feb., 1863; absent sick from Jan., 1865, until April; mustered out June 9, 1865. Died April 6, 1889. Buried at Harrington Cemetery, Route 116, Scituate, Rhode Island.

Sergeant Peter A. Marsh. Moulder. Residence, Providence; enrolled Aug. 8, 1862; mustered in Sept. 6; discharged at Portsmouth Grove Hospital by order May 5, 1863.

Sergeant Henry M. Richter. Clerk. Residence, Providence. Transferred from Co. G, Sept. 1, 1864; sergeant-major Nov. 4, 1864.

Corporal John F. Austin. Carder. Residence, Scituate; enrolled Aug. 8, 1862; mustered in Sept. 6; wounded at Fredericksburg Dec. 13, 1862, and sent to Portsmouth Grove Hospital; discharged on surgeon's certificate at Providence, March 13, 1863. Died December 17, 1886. Buried at Rockland Cemetery, Route 102, Scituate, Rhode Island.

Corporal Patrick Hackett. Peddler. Residence, Providence; enrolled Aug. 12, 1862; mustered in Sept. 6; transferred to the Veteran Reserve Corps, Aug 6, 1864; mustered out as of the 19th Co., 2d Battalion of same at Providence, Sept. 6,

1865. Died September 24, 1878. Buried at ACI Cemetery, Route 37, Cranston, Rhode Island.

Corporal Franklin Howland. Cooper. Residence, Providence; enrolled Aug. 8, 1862; mustered in Sept. 6; discharged on surgeon's certificate from U. S. A. General Hospital, Cincinnati, Ohio, Aug. 17, 1864.

Corporal Philander T. Robbins. Farmer. Residence, Foster; enrolled July 8, 1862; mustered in Sept. 6; sergeant March 1, 1863; first sergeant March 1, 1865; mustered out June 9, 1865.

Corporal Roswell H. Potter. Laborer. Residence, Providence; enrolled Aug. 8, 1862; mustered in Sept. 6; absent sick from Nov., 1862, until Jan., 1863; died of Yazoo Fever at Milldale, Miss., July 22, 1863. Buried at Vicksburg National Cemetery, Vicksburg, Mississippi.

Corporal George H. Smith. Jeweler. Residence, Scituate; enrolled Aug. 11, 1862; mustered in Sept. 6; died of typhoid fever near Falmouth, Va., Jan. 3, 1863. Buried at Clayville Cemetery, Route 102, Foster, Rhode Island.

Corporal Fleming Vance. Moulder. Residence, Providence; enrolled Aug. 8, 1862; mustered in Sept. 6; mustered out June 9, 1865.

Corporal George W. Young. Baker. Residence, Providence; enrolled Aug. 8, 1862; mustered in Sept. 6; discharged on surgeon's certificate at Lovell General Hospital, Portsmouth Grove, March 16, 1864. Died March 24, 1891. Buried at West Greenwich Cemetery 43, Pond View Court at Pole 4, West Greenwich, Rhode Island.

Drummer William A. Abbott. Moulder. Residence, Providence; enrolled Aug. 8, 1862; mustered in Sept. 6; mustered out June 9, 1865. Died September 20, 1896. Buried at Moschuck Cemetery, Central Falls, Rhode Island.

Wagoner John A. Austin. Carder. Residence, Smithfield; enrolled Aug. 8, 1862; mustered in Sept. 6; on extra duty in quartermaster's department as teamster from Nov., 1862, until Feb., 1863; in quartermaster's department from April, 1865 to June, 1865; mustered out June 9, 1865. Died 1916. Buried at East Greenwich Cemetery, First Avenue, East Greenwich, Rhode Island.

Ashworth, William. Sailor. Residence, Coventry; enrolled Aug. 15, 1862; mustered in Sept. 6; sent from Milldale, Miss., to Covington, Ky.; sick Aug. 1, 1863; died in hospital at Lexington, Ky., Jan. 30, 1864. Buried at St. Phillip's Cemetery, Church Street, West Warwick, Rhode Island.

Ayelsworth, Albert H. Farmer. Residence, Scituate; enrolled Aug. 14, 1862; mustered in Sept. 6; absent sick at City Point, Va., Jan., 1865, and borne as absent sick until May 31, 1865, when mustered out at Washington, D. C.

Battey, Hiram S. Farmer. Residence, Johnston; enrolled Aug. 8, 1862; mustered in Sept. 6; died of disease at Marine Hospital, Cincinnati, Ohio, Aug. 16, 1863, while temporarily attached to Battery E, 2d U. S. Artillery. Buried at Camp Denison National Cemetery, Cincinnati, Ohio.

Bateman, George. Spinner. Residence, Providence; enrolled Aug. 14, 1862; mustered in Sept. 6; on detached service in hospital from Nov., 1862, until Jan., 1863; absent sick from July 4, 1863, until Aug. 20, 1863, when he died at General

Hospital, Covington, Ky. Buried at Nicholasville National Cemetery, Nicholasville, Kentucky.

Bigelow, Edward. Laborer. Residence, Woonsocket; enrolled Aug. 17, 1862; mustered in Sept. 6; mustered out June 9, 1865.

Briggs, James A. Farmer. Residence, Foster; enrolled Aug. 18, 1862; mustered in Sept. 6; absent sick at Pleasant Valley, Md., from Oct. 27, 1862, until Jan., 1863; discharged for disability at West's Building Hospital, Baltimore, Md. Died September 9, 1896. Buried at Foster Cemetery 65, South Killingly Road, Foster, Rhode Island.

Brown, John D. Farmer. Residence, North Providence; enrolled Aug. 8, 1862; mustered in Sept. 6; transferred to Veteran Reserve Corps, Jan. 15, 1864; mustered out as of Co. C, 3d Regiment, of same, July 12, 1865. Died 1917. Buried at Oak Grove Cemetery, Central Ave, Pawtucket, Rhode Island.

Bryden, Wilson C. Sailor. Residence, Burrillville; enrolled Aug. 6, 1862; mustered in Sept.; discharged on surgeon's certificate at Philadelphia, Pa., Nov. 14, 1862; (said to have been a musician, to have served originally in Co. D, and to have been transferred Oct. 14, 1862). Buried at Mt. Zion Cemetery, Webster, Massachusetts.

Bunn, James A. Farmer. Residence, Glocester; enrolled Aug. 18, 1862; mustered in Sept. 6; mustered out June 9, 1865.

Clarke, Stephen A. Farmer. Residence, Hopkinton; enrolled Aug. 25, 1862; mustered in Sept. 4; killed in action near Poplar Spring Church, Va., Sept. 30, 1864. Remains interred in Poplar Grove National Cemetery, Petersburg, Virginia.

Memorial stone at Wood River Cemetery, Route 3, Richmond, Rhode Island.

Cole, Henry S. Farmer. Residence, Foster; enrolled Aug. 16, 1862; mustered in Sept. 6; killed at Fredericksburg Dec. 13, 1862. Buried at Pole 53, Central Pike, Foster, Rhode Island.

Cole, John H. Residence, Scituate; enrolled Aug. 8, 1862; mustered in Sept. 6; mustered out June 9, 1865; died at Hope on September 26, 1865 of disease contracted in the service. Buried at Scituate Cemetery 59, Field Hill Road, Scituate, Rhode Island.

Collins, Charles H. Spinner. Residence, North Mansfield, Mass.; enrolled at Providence, July 18, 1862; mustered in Sept. 6; wounded severely in thigh in action near Petersburg June 26, 1864; mustered out June 9, 1865. Died October 29, 1892. Buried at North Burial Ground, Providence, Rhode Island.

Collins, Nehemiah R. Farmer. Residence, Scituate; enrolled Aug. 8, 1862; mustered in Sept. 6; wounded at Fredericksburg Dec. 13, 1862; discharged for disability at Portsmouth Grove Feb. 2, 1864. Died August 8, 1888. Buried at Pole 58, Seven Mile Road, Scituate, Rhode Island.

Colvin, Charles F. Farmer. Residence, Scituate; enrolled Aug. 8, 1862; mustered in Sept. 6; sergeant June 1, 1863; mustered out June 9, 1865. Died Nov. 19, 1879. Buried at Greenwood Cemetery, Fairview Avenue, Coventry, Rhode Island.

Colwell, George. Farmer. Residence, Johnston; enrolled Aug. 8, 1862; mustered in Sept. 6; mustered out June 9,

1865. Died July 12, 1912. Buried at Knotty Oak Cemetery, Route 117, Coventry, Rhode Island.

Corbin, Amasa N. Laborer. Residence, Scituate; enrolled Aug. 19, 1862; mustered in Sept. 6; died of typhoid near Falmouth, Va., Dec. 24, 1862. Buried at Clayville Cemetery, Route 102, Foster, Rhode Island.

Corbin, William H. Farmer. Residence, Scituate; enrolled Aug. 19, 1862; mustered in Sept. 6; slightly wounded in head in action near Petersburg, Va., June 8, 1864; mustered out June 9, 1865. Died December 26, 1922. Buried at Walnut Hill Cemetery, Armistice Boulevard, Pawtucket, Rhode Island.

Cornell, Ira. Farmer. Residence, Coventry; enrolled Aug. 14, 1862; mustered in Sept. 6; wounded at Fredericksburg Dec. 13, 1862; deserted at Cincinnati, Ohio., April 1, 1863. Buried at Pine Tree Cemetery, Route 117, Coventry, Rhode Island.

Cornell, Ira, Jr. Farmer. Residence, Coventry; enrolled Aug. 15, 1862; mustered in Sept. 6; discharged for disability at Portsmouth Grove, Oct. 14, 1864. Died April 29, 1867. Buried at Pine Tree Cemetery, Route 117, Coventry, Rhode Island.

Corey, Charles H. Spinner. Residence, North Providence; enrolled Aug. 8, 1862; mustered in Sept. 6; died of Yazoo Fever at Camp Denison, Ohio Sept. 15, 1863. Buried at Camp Denison National Cemetery, Cincinnati, Ohio.

Cummings, Chester C. Farmer. Residence, Foster; enrolled Aug. 8, 1862; mustered in Sept. 6; transferred to Co. F, 17th Regiment, Veteran Reserve Corps, Oct. 31, 1863; mustered out as of same June 30, 1865. Died 1874. Buried at North Burial Ground, Providence, Rhode Island.

Earle, Albert. Carpenter. Residence, Scituate; enrolled Aug. 14, 1862; mustered in Sept. 6; wounded at Fredericksburg Dec. 13, 1862, and sent to hospital; transferred to the Invalid Corps by order dated Sept. 1, 1863; mustered out as of the 19th Co., 2d Battalion, Veteran Reserve Corps, Sept. 6, 1865.

Farnham, Samuel. Clerk. Residence, Uxbridge, Mass.; enrolled at Scituate Aug. 8, 1862; mustered in Sept. 6; corporal Jan. 4, 1863; sergeant June 4, 1863; appointed captain in the 14th R.I. Heavy Artillery, and discharged to accept the appointment by order dated Dec. 22, 1863; lost at sea Oct. 15, 1865.

Farrow, Enos. Farmer. Residence, Foster; enrolled Aug. 16, 1862; mustered in Sept. 6; absent sick at Washington, from Nov. 17, 1862, until Dec. 3, 1862, when he died in hospital of typhoid. Buried at the Soldier's Home, Washington, D.C.

Field, George A. Farmer. Residence, Scituate; enrolled Aug. 8, 1862; mustered in Sept. 6; absent sick in hospital from Oct. 27, 1862, until Nov. 9, 1862; sick in hospital from Aug. 28, 1863, until Sept. 17, 1863; died of dysentery at general hospital, Lexington, Ky., April 5, 1864. Buried at Scituate Cemetery 59, Field Hill Road, Scituate, Rhode Island.

Gavitt, James W. Farmer. Residence, Coventry; enrolled Aug. 14, 1862; mustered in Sept. 6; wounded slightly in hand in action before Petersburg, June 16, 1864; wounded in battle near Weldon Railroad, Sept. 30, 1864; mustered out June 9, 1865. Died Jan. 19, 1895. Buried at Manchester Cemetery, Coventry, Rhode Island.

Greene, Lewis E. Farmer. Residence, Scituate; enrolled Aug. 8, 1862; mustered in Sept. 6; discharged from West's Building Hospital, Baltimore, Md., on surgeon's certificate June 20, 1863. Died June 4, 1910. Buried at Acoates Hill Cemetery, Route 44, Glocester, Rhode Island.

Hackett, John. Residence, Providence; enrolled Aug. 8, 1862; mustered in Sept. 6; corporal June 4, 1863; on Color Guard; mustered out June 9, 1865. Died May 14, 1867. Buried at Swan Point Cemetery, Providence, Rhode Island.

Harkness, Henry A. Carpenter. Residence, Coventry; enrolled Aug. 14, 1862; mustered in Sept. 6; severely wounded in abdomen before Petersburg June 26, 1864, and sent to hospital; discharged on surgeon's certificate Jan. 26, 1865. Died in 1880. Buried at Manchester Cemetery, Route 117, Coventry, Rhode Island.

Harrington, William O. Farmer. Residence, Foster; enrolled Aug. 14, 1862; mustered in Sept. 6; mustered out June 9, 1865. Died March 18, 1904. Buried at Moosup Cemetery, Moosup Valley Road, Foster, Rhode Island.

Hawkins, George W. Spinner. Residence, Scituate; enrolled Aug. 14, 1862; mustered in Sept. 6; mustered out June 9, 1865. Died August 5, 1909. Buried at Rockland Cemetery, Route 102, Scituate, Rhode Island.

Hill, Charles E. Gilder. Residence, Providence; enrolled at Newport Aug. 18, 1862; mustered in Sept. 6, 1862; mustered out June 9, 1865; died at Chicago. Buried in Chicago, Illinois.

Holloway, Thomas T. Farmer. Residence, Foster; enrolled Aug. 16, 1862; mustered in Sept. 6; absent sick from July 4,

1863, until Aug. 23, 1863, when he died at Union Hospital, Memphis, Tenn. Buried at Winsor Cemetery, Winsor Road, Foster, Rhode Island.

Hopkins, Adoniram J. Farmer. Residence, Foster; enrolled Aug. 12, 1862; mustered in Sept. 6; discharged for disability at Baltimore, Md., March 4, 1863. Died April 7, 1930. Buried at Hopkins Mills Cemetery, Route 6, Foster, Rhode Island.

Hopkins, Asel A. Farmer. Residence, Foster; enrolled Aug. 9, 1862; mustered in Sept. 6; died at Loudon, Tenn., April 11, 1864. Buried at Nashville National Cemetery, Nashville, Tennessee.

Hopkins, Darius A. Farmer. Residence, Scituate; enrolled Aug. 16, 1862; mustered in Sept. 6; left sick at Cairo, Ill, Aug. 17, 1863; discharged from Camp Denison, Ohio, Sept. 29, 1863; died before he left the camp. Buried at Clayville Cemetery, Route 102, Foster, Rhode Island.

Hopkins, John. Farmer. Residence, Foster; enrolled Aug. 16, 1862; mustered in Sept. 6; died in regimental hospital at Newport News, Va., March 1, 1863. Buried at Pole 11, Walker Road, Foster, Rhode Island.

Hopkins, John E. Farmer. Residence, Foster; enrolled Aug. 12, 1862; mustered in Sept. 6; died at Memphis, Tenn., Aug. 17, 1863. Buried at Hopkins Mills Cemetery, Route 6, Foster, Rhode Island.

Hopkins, William D. Residence, Providence; enrolled at Scituate Aug. 9, 1862; mustered in Sept. 6; sergeant June 8, 1863; died in Providence, while on furlough Oct. 4, 1863. Buried at Swan Point Cemetery, Providence, Rhode Island.

Jordan, John F. Overseer. Residence, Scituate; enrolled Aug. 8, 1862; mustered in Sept. 6; on detached service at division headquarters Jan., 1863; mustered out June 9, 1865. Died January 14, 1905. Buried at Glenford Cemetery, Danielson Pike, Scituate, Rhode Island.

Jordan, William H. Farmer. Residence, Coventry; enrolled Aug. 11, 1862; mustered in Sept. 6; in quartermaster's department from Jan., 1865, until June, 1865; mustered out June 9, 1865. Buried at Knotty Oak Cemetery, Coventry, Rhode Island.

Keach, Henry M. Farmer. Residence, Blackstone, Mass.; enrolled at Cumberland June 27, 1862; mustered in Sept. 6; deserted at Pleasant Valley, Md., Oct. 10, 1862.

Kelley, Michael R. Laborer. Residence, Scituate; enrolled Aug. 8, 1862; mustered in Sept. 6; absent with leave for fifteen days March, 1865; mustered out June 9, 1865. Died September 4, 1870. Buried at Saint Patrick's Cemetery, Sixth Avenue, Providence, Rhode Island.

Kenny, Steakley. Farmer. Residence, Richmond; enrolled Aug. 26, 1862; mustered in Sept. 6; on detached service in ambulance corps from Nov., 1862, until Feb., 1863; mustered out June 9, 1865.

Kenyon, Abel B. Spinner Residence, Hopkinton; enrolled Aug. 25, 1862; mustered in Sept. 6; slightly wounded in head at battle near Jackson, Miss., July 13, 1863; slightly wounded in hand at Spotsylvania, May 12, 1864; absent sick at Philadelphia, Jan., 1865; mustered out June 9, 1865. Died November 28, 1911. Buried at Rockville Cemetery, Route 138, Hopkinton, Rhode Island.

Knight, Jeremiah F. Farmer. Residence, West Greenwich; enrolled Aug. 8, 1862; mustered in Sept. 6; on ambulance corps from Nov., 1862, until Feb., 1863, and also from Jan., 1865, until June; mustered out June 9, 1865. Died September 23, 1903. Buried at Knotty Oak Cemetery, Route 117, Coventry, Rhode Island.

Lewis, Edward S. Laborer. Residence, Scituate; enrolled Aug. 8, 1862; mustered in Sept. 6; wounded at Spotsylvania May 18, 1864; absent sick at Portsmouth Grove Hospital from Jan., 1865, until June 14, 1865, when he reported from hospital and was mustered out to date June 9, 1865. Died December 29, 1920. Buried at Brayton Cemetery, Route One, Warwick, Rhode Island.

Lillibridge, Charles P. Shoemaker Residence, Scituate; enrolled Aug. 8, 1862; mustered in Sept. 6; discharged on surgeon's certificate at Newport News, Va., March 19, 1863. Died April 20, 1889. Buried at Exeter Cemetery 6, Summit Road, Exeter, Rhode Island.

Maxon, Joel C. Farmer. Residence, Hopkinton; enrolled Aug. 25, 1862; mustered in Sept. 6; absent sick from Nov. 17, 1862, until Feb., 1863; discharged at Louisville, Ky., Aug. 13, 1863. Died of illness contracted in the service at Hopkinton, Rhode Island on September 24, 1863. Buried at Oak Grove Cemetery, Route 3, Hopkinton, Rhode Island.

Nye, Charles P. Clerk. Residence, Richmond; enrolled Aug. 26, 1862; mustered in Sept. 6; corporal April 4, 1863; slightly wounded in thigh before Petersburg July 8, 1864; mustered out June 9, 1865. Buried at Wood River Cemetery, Richmond, Rhode Island.

Nye, Isaac. Carpenter. Residence, Coventry; enrolled Aug. 14, 1862; mustered in Sept. 6; corporal on Color Guard; wounded at Spotsylvania, May 18, 1864; died of wounds in hospital at Alexandria, Va., May 30, 1864. Buried at Manchester Cemetery, Route 117, Coventry, Rhode Island.

Parker, Joseph. Laborer. Residence, Cranston; enrolled Aug. 8, 1862; mustered in Sept. 6; wounded at Spotsylvania May 12, 1864; mustered out June 9, 1865.

Perry, Joseph B. Clerk. Residence, Richmond; enrolled Aug. 26, 1862; mustered in Sept. 6; absent sick from Oct. 27, 1862, until Jan. 27, 1863, when he was discharged at Convalescent Camp, Va. Died September 16, 1908. Buried at Pine Grove Cemetery, Bank Street, Hopkinton, Rhode Island.

Pierce, Benjamin H. Farmer. Residence, Scituate; enrolled Aug. 11, 1862; mustered in Sept. 6; mustered out June 9, 1865. Buried at Clayville Cemetery, Route 102, Foster, Rhode Island.

Pierce, Edwin O. Spinner. Residence, Scituate; enrolled Aug. 8, 1862; mustered in Sept. 6; transferred to Veteran Reserve Corps, Jan. 28, 1865; mustered out as of Co. H, 19th Regiment of same July 13, 1865. Died 1914. Buried at West Warwick Cemetery 26, Parker Street, West Warwick, Rhode Island.

Potter, George H. Blacksmith. Residence, Foster; enrolled Aug. 14, 1862; mustered in Sept. 6; wounded at Fredericksburg Dec. 13, 1862; corporal June 4, 1863; wounded slightly in hand in action near Cold Harbor, Va., June 8, 1864; sergeant March 1, 1865; mustered out June 9,

1865. Died January 28, 1909. Buried at Sterling Cemetery, Route 14-A, Sterling, Connecticut.

Potter, Pardon K. Stage Driver. Residence, Cranston; enrolled Aug. 4, 1862; mustered in Sept. 6; left sick at Pleasant Valley, Md., Oct. 27, 1862; discharged on surgeon's certificate at Portsmouth Grove, March 24, 1863. Died January 10, 1913. Buried at Cottrell Cemetery, Seven Mile Road, Scituate, Rhode Island.

Pray, Esius. Farmer. Residence, Foster; enrolled Aug. 14, 1862; mustered in Sept. 6; jaw severely fractured at Spotsylvania Court House May 12, 1864, and sent to General Hospital; discharged on surgeon's certificate at Portsmouth Grove Nov. 17, 1864.

Reynolds, Edward S. Farmer. Residence, Scituate; enrolled Aug. 14, 1862; mustered in Sept. 6; corporal April 4, 1863; killed in action near Mechanicsville, Va., June 2, 1864. Buried at Cold Harbor National Cemetery, Cold Harbor, Virginia.

Roberts, Henry A. Farmer. Residence, Warwick; enrolled July, 1862; mustered in Sept. 6; on extra duty in quartermaster's department from Nov., 1862, until Feb., 1863; wounded slightly in arm in action near Petersburg June 29, 1864; mustered out June 9, 1865. Buried at Cranston Cemetery 7, Pippin Orchard Road, Cranston, Rhode Island.

Rounds, Chester P. Farmer. Residence, Foster; enrolled Aug. 16, 1862; mustered in Sept. 6; wounded at Spotsylvania Court House, May 12, 1864, and sent to hospital; absent sick at Portsmouth Grove from Jan. 1, 1865, until March or May, 1865, when he was transferred to Veteran Reserve Corps; mustered out as of 2d Battalion of same July 18, 1865. Died in 1925. Buried at Pocasset Cemetery, Dyer Avenue, Cranston, Rhode Island.

Salisbury, Alpheus. Weaver. Residence, Scituate; enrolled Aug. 8, 1862; mustered in Sept. 6; severely wounded at Fredericksburg Dec. 13, 1862, and sent to hospital; discharged on surgeon's certificate at Providence, March 19, 1863. Died of wounds at Providence, Rhode Island July 4, 1863. Buried at Clayville Cemetery, Route 102, Foster, Rhode Island.

Searle, Benjamin F. Clothier. Residence, Cranston; enrolled Aug. 5, 1862; mustered in Sept. 6; left sick at Baltimore March 26, 1863; discharged on certificate of disability at Cincinnati, Ohio, Dec. 30, 1863. Buried in Cranston Cemetery 8, located at telephone pole 72, Seven Mile Road, Cranston, Rhode Island.

Searle, Henry E. Weaver. Residence, Scituate; enrolled Aug. 8, 1862; mustered in Sept. 6; absent sick at Portsmouth Grove from Jan., 1865, until May 20, when he was transferred to the Veteran Reserve Corps; mustered out as of Co. E, 12th Regiment of same, June 27, 1865.

Shippee, Horace J. Farmer. Residence, Foster; enrolled Aug. 14, 1862; mustered in Sept. 6; on detached service at division headquarters from Dec., 1862, until Feb., 1863; in corps commissary department from Jan., 1865, until May, 1865; mustered out June 9. Died November 15, 1894. Buried at Elm Grove Cemetery, North Kingstown, Rhode Island.

Simmons, George. Farmer. Residence, Foster; enrolled Aug. 14, 1862; mustered in Sept. 6; wounded at Fredericksburg Dec. 13, 1862; sent to Portsmouth Grove Hospital and borne as absent sick until Feb., 1863; killed at Spotsylvania May

12, 1864. Buried at Foster Cemetery 54, Central Pike, Foster, Rhode Island.

Simmons, John. Farmer. Residence, Smithfield; enrolled Aug. 6, 1862; mustered in Sept. 6; wounded and sent to Washington on Dec. 13, 1862; deserted from camp near Falmouth, Va., Jan. 24, 1863.

Simmons, Isaac. Farmer. Residence, Foster; enrolled Aug. 14, 1862; mustered in Sept. 6; mustered out June 9, 1865. Buried at Pocasset Cemetery, Dyer Avenue, Cranston, Rhode Island.

Smith, James T. Carder. Residence, North Providence; enrolled Aug. 8, 1862; mustered in Sept. 6; absent with leave for fifteen days Jan., 1865; mustered out June 9, 1865.

Smith, Joseph. Spinner. Residence, North Providence; enrolled and mustered in Nov. 3, 1863; wounded in abdomen near Petersburg, Va., June 27, 1864; mustered out as of Co. G, July 13, 1865.

Studley, John N. Teamster. Residence, Scituate; enrolled Aug. 14, 1862; mustered in Sept. 6; wounded at Fredericksburg Dec. 13, 1862, and sent to hospital; discharged at Providence, April 3, 1862. Died March 13, 1879. Buried at Coventry Cemetery 81 at Pole 5, Kilton Lane, Coventry, Rhode Island.

Taylor, James J. Laborer. Residence, Smithfield; enrolled Aug. 15, 1862; mustered in Sept. 6; died in Finley Hospital, Washington, D. C., July 6, 1864, of wounds received in action at Cold Harbor, June 6, 1864. Buried at Arlington National Cemetery.

Thurston, Caleb. Farmer. Residence, Richmond; enrolled Aug. 23, 1862; mustered in Sept. 6; left sick at Covington, Ky., Aug. 23, 1863; discharged at Portsmouth Grove on surgeon's certificate Feb. 29, 1864. Died May 15, 1883. Buried at Wood River Cemetery, Route 3, Richmond, Rhode Island.

Waterman, Albert G. Peddler. Residence, Cranston; enrolled Aug. 11, 1862; mustered in Sept. 6; mustered out June 9, 1865. Died May 15, 1897. Buried at Buried at Waterman Lot, Route 6 at Pole 107, Johnston, Rhode Island.

Weigand, Frederick. Merchant. Residence, Worcester, Mass.; enrolled at Providence Aug. 24, 1862; color sergeant Oct. 13; second lieutenant Co. G, Jan. 7, 1863.

Whiting, Hassan O. Farmer. Residence, Smithfield; mustered in Sept. 6; transferred to Veteran Reserve Corps March 16, 1864; mustered out as of Co. K, 5th Regiment of same, June 30, 1865.

Williams, Olney D. Stone Cutter. Residence, North Providence; enrolled Aug. 9, 1862; mustered in Sept. 6; killed in action at Fredericksburg, Dec. 13, 1862. Buried at Fredericksburg National Cemetery, Fredericksburg National Cemetery.

Winsor, Albert A. Farmer. Residence, Foster; enrolled Aug. 16, 1862; mustered in Sept. 6; killed at Fredericksburg Dec. 13, 1862. Buried at Winsor Cemetery, Winsor Road, Foster, Rhode Island.

Wood, Oliver. Carpenter. Residence, Sterling, Ct.; enrolled at Foster Aug. 14, 1862; mustered in Sept. 6; died at Washington, D. C., June 15, 1864, of wounds received at

Cold Harbor June 3. Buried at Lime Cemetery, South Killingly Road, Foster, Rhode Island.

Young, Searles B. Farmer. Residence, Foster; enrolled Aug. 14, 1862; mustered in Sept. 6; wounded at Fredericksburg Dec. 13, 1862; sent to hospital and borne as absent sick until Feb. 4, 1863, when he was discharged at Washington, D. C., on account of wounds. Died August 12, 1925. Buried at North Foster Cemetery, Paine Road, Foster, Rhode Island.

Bibliographical Notes

The above work was written by the veterans of Company K, Seventh Rhode Island Volunteers. This editor has simply annotated the work for the reader. For this task this editor has freely used William P. Hopkins, *The History of the Seventh Rhode Island Volunteers, 1862-1865*. This is one of the best of the hundreds of regimental histories written after the Civil War. It reads in almost a diary format and contains biographical sketches and images of hundreds of members of the regiment. In addition the muster rolls are far more proficient then those in the *Revised Register of Rhode Island Volunteers*. The tome was published in 1893 and is a revised record of all of the Rhode Islanders that served in the Civil War. In addition almost every Rhode Island regiment wrote a regimental history which was of immense use to follow the path of the Rhode Islanders in the Civil War. In recent years, the two books of Kris VanDenBossche, *Pleas excuse all bad writing* and *Write soon and give me all the news* provide the reader with an excellent source of transcribed letters of Rhode Island's Civil War soldiers.

The Rhode Island Historical Society in Providence is a great repository of Civil War records. In their possession are thousands of letters and diaries, many untouched by historians to narrate the story. The Rhode Island State House contains the Rhode Island battle flags and other Civil War relics. In addition the Rhode Island State Archives is the official repository for Rhode Island's state records for the Civil War, including enlistment records and quartermaster records. Furthermore, almost every town in Rhode Island has a historical society, many of which have Civil War material. Of particular note is the Pettaquamscutt Historical Society in

South Kingstown. This editor has used all of these records to help annotate this work.

Another resource that was used was the historical cemeteries of Rhode Island. In these long forgotten graveyards in the woods, this editor was able to study the men of Company K and gain knowledge of their families. Unfortunately Rhode Island has thousands of these small cemeteries, many of which are neglected on unpaved roads in rural Rhode Island. In addition the town records of Rhode Island's towns provide vital genealogical material to study not only the men whom fought, but the families and communities these men left behind.

Through a study such as this the voices of the past live on, and the Rhode Islanders who went south to preserve the Union continue to speak.

About the Author

Robert Grandchamp is a history graduate student at Rhode Island College where he received a BA in American History and Anthropology. He is the author of *"With their usual ardor:" Scituate, Rhode Island and the American Revolution* and *The Seventh Rhode Island Infantry in the Civil War*, in addition to numerous other historical monographs. The recipient of the 2007 Margaret B. Stillwell award for book collecting, he resides in Warwick, Rhode Island.

www.ingramcontent.com/pod-product-compliance
Lightning Source LLC
Chambersburg PA
CBHW050814160426
43192CB00010B/1759